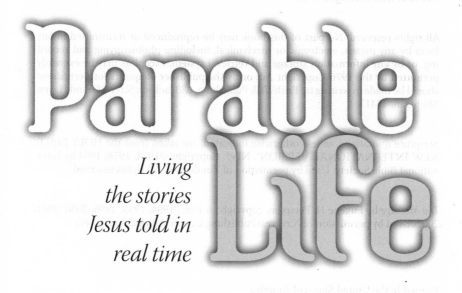

Parable Life

*Living
the stories
Jesus told in
real time*

MICHELLE VAN LOON

D1531663

FaithWalk

PUBLISHING

Grand Haven, MI 49417

©2005 Michelle Van Loon
Published by FaithWalk Publishing
Grand Haven, Michigan 49417

Scripture quotations, unless otherwise indicated, are taken from the HOLY BIBLE, NEW INTERNATIONAL VERSION®. NIV®. Copyright ©1973, 1978, 1984 by International Bible Society. Used by permission of Zondervan. All rights reserved.

The Message by Eugene H. Peterson, copyright © 1993, 1994, 1995, 1996, 2000, 2001, 2002. Used by permission of NavPressPublishing Group. All rights reserved.

Printed in the United States of America

10 09 08 07 06 05   7 6 5 4 3 2 1

Library of Congress Cataloging-in-Publication Data

Van Loon, Michelle.
ParableLife : living the stories of Jesus in real time / by Michelle Van Loon.
    p. cm.
Includes bibliographical references.
ISBN-13: 978-1-932902-55-6 (pbk. : alk. paper)
ISBN-10: 1-932902-55-4
1. Jesus Christ—Parables. 2. Christian life. I. Title.
BT375.3.V36 2005
226.8'06—dc22
        2005015121

Dedication

To Meg,

*who called me at 7 a.m. one morning a few years ago
to sing me back to life
and has been singing God's stories to me ever since.*

Contents

Acknowledgments

My husband Bill, who has lived these stories with me for over a quarter century and counting, has had to live through the writing of them in recent months, and actually seemed to enjoy all of it. Anyone who has ever lieved with a writer knows this is no small thing. There is not a better travel companion, lover, hero, and friend on the globe.

Rachel and Carlos (and amazin' toddler Gabriel), Ben, and Jacob have lived a lot of these stories with me, too. God is using your lives to writ his story in creative ways. I am proud of each one of you.

Meg Kausalik and Kathy Bogacz, two women who write way better than I do, provided input, correction, hard-core prayer, and more than a little cheerleading along the journey. How do yo say thanks for stuff like that? (Thanks.) Amy Pomplin, Kristina Scott, and Dan and Maribeth Van Loon lent helpful eyes to parts of the process, too.

I am in awe of the invisible army of Annas that serve in houses of prayer all over the globe. My life has been changed because of you. Special thanks go to Chicago's Prayer Furnace and www.thenightwatch.com.

The conversations I've had with many of my coworkers at Trinity International University's bookstore during this writing process have been life-giving.

A big shout out goes to my writing students, past and present. I'm positive that you've all taught me more than I ever taught you guys.

Starbucks coffee is even good if you drink it at room temperature at one in the afternoon while you're still in your jammies. Or so I've heard.

Dirk Wierenga of Faithwalk Publishers, you believed in me. Wow.

Jesus. I have no words to express how wonderful you are, my Savior. I love you.

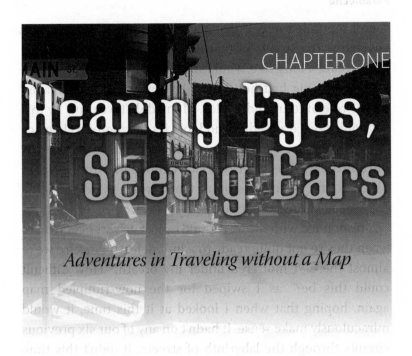

CHAPTER ONE

Hearing Eyes, Seeing Ears

Adventures in Traveling without a Map

How difficult could it be?

"You guys, we've got to do a quick run to the post office. This shouldn't take more than fifteen minutes max," I told my three school-age kids. "This'll give us a chance to take a quick peek at our new hometown. Grab your coats."

Our family had relocated from Chicago to Waukesha, a small city near Milwaukee, Wisconsin, just three days earlier. We jumped into our beat-up van, and I paused to study the city map and figure out where we were going. The post office, near the center of town, located in a spaghetti bowl of random, crazily plotted streets. The effect was as if someone had taken the scribblings of an angry toddler and decided that one of the crazed crayon drawings would make an ideal layout for a city. For a nervous moment, I wondered whether this trip would be quite as simple as I'd billed it, but then I reminded myself that I was a veteran Chicago driver, navigating the streets of that city like a cabbie. Finding my way around a burg like Waukesha would be a cinch.

A frustrating half hour later, 10-year-old Ben had taken on the role of tour guide. "Hey, Mom, didn't we drive by this vet's office twice already? And look, it's the motorcycle place again. Those are cool dirt bikes. I want a dirt bike for my next birthday." The other two kids chimed in with their own observations. "Can we stop at that Hardee's and get some fries the next time we drive by it?"

I responded with the words said by lost drivers everywhere when they're not quite ready to admit defeat: "I'm sure we're almost there." I muttered under my breath, "How difficult could this be?" as I swiped for the now-rumpled map again, hoping that when I looked at it this time, it would miraculously make sense. It hadn't on any of our six previous circuits through the labyrinth of streets. It didn't this time, either. Ready to admit defeat, I pulled into the parking lot next to the vet's office to try to get my bearings.

Ben asked pointedly, "Are we lost?"

I told him, no, we weren't exactly lost, but that, apparently, someone had misplaced the post office. I flagged down a passerby and asked him for directions. The man laughed wickedly and said, "Oh, you can't get there from here." He then launched into a series of directions so complicated that not even a civil engineer would understand them. I gamely asked clarifying questions. The man seemed to believe that I understood what to do next, and left me with these ominous words: "Yeah, Waukesha's streets are crazy, but it was worse when these was all one way streets down here. It's better since they turned most of 'em into two-way streets a coupla years ago."

Better? I couldn't imagine how these streets could have been even more confusing. I smiled weakly, thanked him for the help he thought he gave me, and dove back into the spaghetti bowl. Hot tears of frustration strayed down my face.

It had gotten really, really quiet in the back seat. I glanced in my rearview mirror and realized the kids were watching me with the kind of intense concern that told me that maybe this trip was about more than just mailing a package and buying some stamps. They needed to know that we'd all learn together how to navigate life in this strange new place.

I needed to know the same thing.

I bit my lip, forced my tears back inside of me, and smiled weakly. "Okay, we're a little lost, and it's more than a little frustrating. I know that there's a basic law of physics that says that matter doesn't disappear into thin air," I told them. "It just changes form. Maybe the post office has turned into a pumpkin or birdhouse or something."

It was a stupid joke, but it was enough to cut the tension, and two of them giggled. Minutes later, I stopped a lady outside the Hardee's we'd managed to find for the seventh time. She dictated another set of unintelligible directions.

I admitted defeat and accidentally figured out how to get back to our new home. I never found the post office that day. How difficult could it be?

Later, I learned I had driven past it at least two or three times. I was so disoriented from doing circuits around the tangle of streets that I'd lost sight of what I was searching for.

For a long time, I have felt like I'm reliving that frustrating trip round and round Waukesha when it comes to my life as a follower of Jesus. I've been a part of a variety of different Christian faith communities ranging from hardcore fundamentalist to freestyle charismatic to old school liturgical to pop evangelical. I've tried to use the helpful maps that various expert tour guides have handed to me with the promise of a less messy journey through life: sermons, books, small group bible studies, and lots of confident-sounding advice.

But I keep looping past the same scenery again and again ... and again ... like I've been belted into a slow-moving centrifuge. How did the colorful maps and helpful direction-givers become a substitute for following the one who promised to be my straight, narrow path, leading me home?

Jesus could have given his followers a map showing the route from here to eternity that would have offered us a nice, neat shortcut straight through the complex tangle of life.

Instead, all he says is, "Follow me."

At the height of his celebrity, Jesus had crowds tracking him like thundering herds of lost sheep. A pretty sizable percentage of the herd was there for the show: Theater of the supernatural included dramatic healings and deliverances, raw truth, and tangible, fiery love. The crowds cheered it all. If Jesus were going to pass out maps, this moment in the spotlight would have been the time.

Instead, Jesus told the crowds parables. Parables, by definition, are little bursts of story that paint a picture of an everyday object or situation in order to help the hearer create an analogy with something else, something deeper. The stories that Jesus told mapped the inside-out, upside-down landscape of his kingdom.

The word "kingdom" conjures images of castles (like the kind they have at Disneyland) and jousting matches in Merrie Olde England. It helped me a lot to learn that most of us in modern times might better understand the kind of kingdom that Jesus was talking about if we thought about it as a revolution. Jesus was showing and telling the crowds about a kingdom-revolution that was nothing less than heaven invading earth, bringing radical transformation to everything it touched, from blind eyes to stone-cold hearts to entire communities.[1]

Jesus's parables were completely familiar and completely subversive to his hearers. The people who flocked to hear him understood how exciting it would be to stumble across buried treasure, how frustrating it could be to wait for justice in the midst of corruption, and how their children behaved at the playground of the local marketplace. He told his stories with the quick, vivid verbal edits of a master film director.

Even though the parables used familiar images, Jesus's hearers gained more questions than answers. What on earth was he really saying? Right there, smack dab in the middle of Israel's occupation by a hostile Roman government, Jesus was inviting people to move into a kingdom that had nothing to do with geographical boundaries and the politics of might and wealth.

The closest he came to giving his hearers a map of this kingdom was sketching short, surprising word-pictures of the revolutionary life to which he was calling them. His hearers didn't get it. Yet Jesus wasn't being intentionally obscure or oppositional. He ached for each person in the crowd to truly see and hear.

Jesus's closest friends pulled him aside at one point to ask him why he insisted on speaking in the secrets of story and mystery: Explain yourself, Jesus.

And so, he did:

---

[1] Muchas gracias to Author David Wenham, who fleshed out the idea of revolution in his really helpful commentary *The Parables of Jesus* (InterVarsity Press, 1989).

The disciples came to him and asked, "Why do you speak to the people in parables?"

He replied, "The knowledge of the secrets of the kingdom of heaven has been given to you, but not to them. Whoever has will be given more, and he will have an abundance. Whoever does not have, even what he has will be taken from him. This is why I speak to them in parables:

"Though seeing, they do not see; though hearing, they do not hear or understand. In them is fulfilled the prophecy of Isaiah:

"'You will be ever hearing but never understanding; you will be ever seeing but never perceiving.

For this people's heart has become calloused; they hardly hear with their ears, and they have closed their eyes.

Otherwise they might see with their eyes, hear with their ears, understand with their hearts and turn, and I would heal them.'"

"But blessed are your eyes because they see, and your ears because they hear. For I tell you the truth, many prophets and righteous men longed to see what you see but did not see it, and to hear what you hear but did not hear it."

—Matthew 13:10–17

Jesus tells his secrets out loud, right there in broad daylight.

He quotes Isaiah, the prophet and friend of God who lived about 600 years prior to Jesus's birth. God had called Isaiah to give the people of Israel the message that they needed to reject the do-it-yourself religion they had been practicing and turn back to him. God knew that most of his people wouldn't respond to that message because their hearts had grown hard.

Isaiah's message, like that of most of the other prophetic voices of the Old Testament, was proclaimed to people who were determined to follow their own carefully mapped routes away from God. His words formed a part of God's promise that salvation from this grim cycle of failure was coming. This promise burned in the hearts of a small, ragged remnant of people who longed to follow God.

So Jesus tells his friends the secret: He is the culmination of the desire of generations of ragged remnants of God-followers. Jesus could hear the turning of their uncalloused hearts toward him as they listened deeply and obediently to his words.

That turning, Jesus says, brings healing. This healing was a hallmark of his revolution. The word for healing that Jesus used (*iaomai*) embraces more than the gift of physical healing. It captures the idea of salvation, of making someone free from sin.

Though Jesus spoke plainly to his disciples, he was telling his secrets in story form to everyone who was willing to turn toward him, hungry to hear. And it turns out that the ones who were best able to understand those secrets were blind and deaf and sick or sleazy or broken or desperate or simply tired of the stranglehold of the mapmakers and tour guides on how to live a life of faith.

So when I turned to him, weary and heartbroken, and told him that I was tired of driving the Indy 500 around the spaghetti bowl of the Christian world, Jesus pulled me close and started telling those stories of his. Those stories that had once been as familiar as old wallpaper have become as urgent and contemporary as graffiti.

His healing has arrived in the form of eyes and ears that are able (at last!) to hear and see his stories being written in the lives of a completely unorthodox assortment of people. Some of them have been faithful companions and friends. The irony wasn't wasted on me that there wasn't a single professional map vendor or tour guide among that collection of people. Healing is also coming to me as I've discovered the way that he tells his story in the lives of those who have acted as my foes. And there's a mutt assortment of others who have dropped into my life when I've least expected it, in some pretty unusual ways, reminding me that God's revolution has the power to invade and transform everything.

God wants to give you the same gift—the healing that comes in the form of eyes that can see and ears that can hear him telling his story to you, through his word, illustrated by the people he's placed in your life. You will hear him telling you about a kingdom populated by blind, deaf, sick, sleazy, broken, desperate, tired people who are living the parable life, learning to follow Jesus, choice by choice.

People just like you and me.

There's no map for how you "should" navigate *ParableLife*. Every chapter tells its own story, so dive in anywhere. Each of this book's ten remaining chapters offers five different ways you can experience some of the stories that Jesus told. Each of these parables deals with the theme of what it means to choose to follow Jesus each step of your journey. These chapters are intended to help you hear, and see, and respond to the story as if you're experiencing it for the first time:

Each chapter includes these sections:

Listen to *the story* Jesus told

Hear that story *reloaded*—a biblically faithful retelling of the same story from a different angle.

Watch the story being crafted in contemporary life in the section called *ParableLife*. Each of these stories is true, though in some cases names and minor details have been changed.

Recognize his story in your life *in real time*. This section of the chapter offers thoughts and ideas you can use to connect his story with your own.

Continue the conversation. Each chapter ends with a question you can use to spark discussion with others.

May each of us receive the gift of hearing eyes and seeing ears. May we turn, and follow him home.

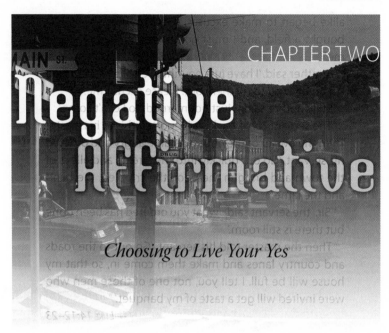

CHAPTER TWO

Negative Affirmative

Choosing to Live Your Yes

The Story of the RSVP

THEN JESUS SAID TO HIS HOST, "When you give a luncheon or dinner, do not invite your friends, your brothers or relatives, or your rich neighbors; if you do, they may invite you back and so you will be repaid. But when you give a banquet, invite the poor, the crippled, the lame, the blind, and you will be blessed. Although they cannot repay you, you will be repaid at the resurrection of the righteous."

When one of those at the table with him heard this, he said to Jesus, "Blessed is the man who will eat at the feast in the kingdom of God."

Jesus replied: "A certain man was preparing a great banquet and invited many guests. At the time of the banquet he sent his servant to tell those who had been invited, 'Come, for everything is now ready.' But they all alike began to make excuses. The first said, 'I have just bought a field, and I must go and see it. Please excuse me.'

"Another said, 'I have just bought five yoke of oxen, and I'm on my way to try them out. Please excuse me.'

"Still another said, 'I just got married, so I can't come.'

"The servant came back and reported this to his master. Then the owner of the house became angry and ordered his servant, 'Go out quickly into the streets and alleys of the town and bring in the poor, the crippled, the blind and the lame.'

"'Sir,' the servant said, 'what you ordered has been done, but there is still room.'

"Then the master told his servant, 'Go out to the roads and country lanes and make them come in, so that my house will be full. I tell you, not one of those men who were invited will get a taste of my banquet.'"

—*Luke 14:12–23*

Reloaded: Engraved Invitation

Jesus had been invited to share a meal at the home of a member of the religious elite. The table was ringed with other religious power brokers. Did they want to simply relax, share a meal, and enjoy some good conversation with Jesus?

Scripture's description of this meal gives the answer: "One Sabbath, when Jesus went to eat in the house of a prominent Pharisee, he was being carefully watched." (Lk 14:1) To most of the religious professionals of the day, Jesus was Trouble. For generations, these guys had served as God's mouthpieces and defense attorneys. Jesus was unimpressed by their power, yet completely committed to inviting them to taste the same love he'd shown to the crowds that gravitated to him. He accepted their invitation even though he knew it was motivated by suspicion, not hospitality.

The appetizer to this Sabbath meal was Jesus breaking one of the cherished rules of his hosts. The forebears of the professionals at the table had spent generations constructing rules beyond those that God had given to them. They believed they were doing God and everyone else a favor by fencing his rules in with lots of other rules. Jesus gently dismantles the fence by healing a man suffering from edema, a painful buildup of fluid in his joints.

As if that wasn't enough, Jesus then goes on to make some pointed comments about the rule-breaking behavior of those assembled around the table. They were used to grabbing places of honor everywhere they went, cutting in line, and getting special treatment. They probably weren't even aware they were breaking rules at this meal.

Until Jesus pointed it out. In the silence that followed, one of the pros at the table broke the silence by saying that those who were invited to join the party in heaven were blessed. His comment seems like an odd silence breaker until you realize that he was saying the words because he was certain that he and the others assembled around the table were going to be honored guests at the ultimate party. Jesus responded to that smug statement with a story about a banquet.

In order to properly plan for food and drink at a large-scale celebration, the host's invitation needs a response from those invited. That way, the host can make sure there's plenty of food and drink for everyone. The RSVP cards that come with most wedding invitations are a perfect example of this courtesy. The first three characters Jesus mentioned in his parable were those formally invited to one amazing party. Each of them had RSVPed to let the host know that they'd be there, bells on.

During a time when people didn't live and die by the tyranny of digital timepieces and Palm Pilots, the way invited guests knew it was time for the festivities to begin was when messengers came huffing and puffing to their homes to tell them to come party.

Jesus tells the religious professionals that this was when the lame excuses showed up instead of the invited guests. Suddenly, garden variety business and family concerns became code-orange emergencies for the guests. Impossible to come to the party today, they all said, things to do, people to see, hair to wash. And this, after they'd committed to attend.

These mean-spirited rejections of the host's generous invitation caused a kind of holy anger to rise up in him. The tables were groaning with food, food that had been gathered at a high cost with much effort, and the absence of these excuse-makers was an insult. They believed that their own wonderful lives were the real party.

This host also knew that there were many whose lives were anything but a party, and he knew this because he'd had his eye on those folks the whole time he was planning his event. In his next breath, he sends his servant out to invite the poor, crippled, lame, and blind ... the people who the religious elite had always smugly classified (and dismissed) as sinners. No excuses from this crowd. They'd heard about parties like this, but had been told by those on the usual guest list that people like them weren't welcome. So when they heard, "Come to a party ... today," nothing could keep this broken crowd from attending.

The host discovers there were still more space and food and drink available, so he invites others. He broadens his invitation to reach people who'd never even heard there was a party going on, but maybe had dreamed of going to a celebration like this. This crowd gladly accepted the invitation, and they had the time of their lives.

Jesus leaves each of us with the same question that his hosts had to answer: If your life already feels like the Best Party Ever, why would you want to leave that party to attend someone else's?

ParableLife: The A List

He found his invitation wadded up in the bottom of his desk drawer that Saturday morning, and nearly tossed it into the pile of useless papers overflowing the trash can. What this paperwork represented seemed life-and-death important at the time, he thought ruefully. There were plans for events such as the church's yearly Easter egg hunt, memos about the decorating wars surrounding the new church lobby, numerous drafts of a new bulletin design for Sunday services. The few files he was packing to bring home compared to the prodigious amount of garbage was a sad metaphor of waste.

Maybe home wasn't quite the right word. He'd be bringing his boxes of books and files to a nearly empty house. His soon-to-be ex-wife had taken most of the furniture with her a week earlier when she'd finished moving out for good. His adult kids had little to do with him these days. Though they were all unceasingly polite when he called, he could feel the potency of their disgust and humiliation. And there was no one to blame for any of it except himself.

How he wished there was someone to scapegoat for this mess, but that illusion had been stripped when his secret was discovered.

He'd spent years cycling between rationalization and remorse. All the while, he felt like he was managing his secret well enough that no one would ever know. It had started with a few curious exposures to *Playboy* and its cousins while he was in Bible college, working second shift at a convenience store/gas station near the interstate.

Everything else in his life at the time was constructed around so many *nos*, and all of those soft-focus Barbies said *yes* to him, page after page. And every time he said *yes* back, there was a release that was the closest thing to joy he had ever experienced.

Afterwards, he'd pour himself on God's mercy and repent. He'd be okay for a while, but when the pressures of life got to be too great, the cycle would begin again. Some relief came when he married a sweet pastor's daughter his last year of school. She was the perfect complement to his goal of career ministry.

When he got a call just after graduation from a church looking for a young assistant, he and his young wife dove eagerly into their lives as Mr. and Mrs. Assistant Pastor. He stayed away from porn for a while, but one night, alone in a distant city at a pastor's conference, he watched one of the fine offerings available on pay-per-view in his hotel room. The magazine had come to life. No one was the wiser.

He was hooked.

A few years later, the head pastor left to take a new position, and he got the job. The church was growing, and the board decided to upgrade to a new computer system that gave the staff unlimited Internet access. The man who installed the system included software that would block objectionable web sites, but it didn't take him long to figure out how he could surf past them to visit a world of virtual *yes*.

He wanted to be a good husband and father and pastor, honestly he did. No one ever would have suspected he had another side to him. He preached good messages and went to his kids' soccer games and ballet recitals and was a dutiful husband. His wife sometimes sensed there was a reserve she couldn't touch in him, but she chalked it up to the busy pace of their lives.

He met the other woman in a chatroom online. This invisible new friend asked nothing of him and understood his need for adventure and *yes*. She lived in a nearby city, not far from his alma mater. It was amazingly easy to arrange a meeting, then another. The spark and fire and illicitness of it all ... the delicious shame ... .

And then there was an audit at the church. He'd gotten a little sloppy, hadn't wiped clean his computer's history regularly. He had spent a little too much money from his discretionary fund to support his habits.

The secret life was no longer a secret. He lost his job. He was facing embezzlement charges. His reputation was ruined, and his wife had moved out. His children couldn't look him in the eye.

And this Saturday morning, cleaning out his office while a couple of the deacons stood guard, at the bottom of the drawer, he found the invitation.

After everything he'd done ... he was still invited?

He wept.

"This house is a mess," she thought wearily. She was exhausted by the thought of doing the kind of cleaning the place really needed. There were sloppy stacks of papers and old magazines piled everywhere. She slid her foot though the sea of Legos that carpeted the floor to make a walkable path between the family room couch and the kitchen.

The kids were asleep. Most of them, anyway. She could see the light on in 15-year-old Jennifer's room, but knew Jen was studying for her history test tomorrow. Kevin had turned in long ago, as had 5-year-old Jeffrey. That Jeffrey went to sleep willingly was nothing short of a miracle. When he'd come to their home as a foster child a year ago, it took hours each night to convince him he was safe and that he was free to fall asleep. Then there was 2-month-old Omar, whose inability to sleep was due to the massive amounts of illegal drugs that had flooded his system while he was in his birth mother's womb.

His birth mom took off from the hospital about six hours after Omar was born. That's when she'd gotten the phone call. The social worker had pleaded. "Please ... there's no one else right now. Please come to the hospital and take him home."

She'd been a foster mom for the last six years, and had cared for six babies in that time. She'd had to let go of each one of them, wrecked inside that most of them were being sent back to precarious situations that some social worker had deemed stable enough to gamble with a baby's life and future. A piece of her heart was torn from her every time.

"You let go of your own son, Father," she'd pray. "You knew he was going into a situation that was going to kill him." And she'd weep and wonder why on earth she kept doing this, especially when her broken heart never seemed to heal but fractured in new places with each child she loved.

Omar stirred, and she sighed. This little one was a tough one. She hadn't had more than a couple of hours of uninterrupted sleep since he entered the household, his nervous system supercharged from a potpourri of drugs.

But for the thousandth time since Omar had appeared in the household, she found herself praying for his birth mom, "Father, forgive her ... because if she knew what she'd done to her little baby ... ."

She looked at Omar, shuddering in his bassinet, hands balled near his face, mouth open in a silent cry in his fitful sleep, looking like Edvard Munch's painting *The Scream*.

She sat down on the couch, hitting the remote and surfing restlessly though the channels. There was the usual menu of infomercials for exercise equipment, weird kitchen appliances, and raunchy *Girls Gone Wild* videos mixed with angry-sounding TV preachers and well coiffed anchors delivering today's bad news. The baby was stirring.

An old magazine from the bottom of one of the mountainous stacks on the coffee table caught her eye, and she pulled it from the pile, hoping to take two minutes to leaf through it before it was Omar Time again.

A piece of construction paper, folded in quarters, lettered in crayon, fell to the floor.

"I'm really going to have to do something about this house ... " she started, for the hundredth time since Omar appeared in their lives eight weeks ago. She bent to pick up the paper.

It was an invitation. It said, "Please bring all the kids."

He stretched and yawned in the darkness of the strip along the highway. The bland sameness of the plastic signs never failed to shock him. It looked like everywhere else he'd ever been. Home Depot, Pizza Hut, Subway, Starbucks, all tucked between quick lube joints and nail salons and dry cleaners and pet supply stores.

He'd been pretty successful at channeling his suburban existential angst into his music. The endless strips of franchise businesses, shiny with promises of consumer fulfillment, left him empty inside.

Home was the same way. There was an intact family once, a shiny strip mall of a family, but then his dad got tired of it and took off with a coworker to build a new strip mall family halfway across the country. His lonely, fractured mom dated a bunch of men, and worked too much, trusting that he and his older sister would find their own way through the rest of their childhoods.

Nothing felt real. Music beckoned him, gave him a place to pour out his anger. The rest of the music scene gave him a way to anesthesize himself after he'd tried to purge some of that anger. The bar fights, the random hookups, the substances aplenty all promised to make the emptiness stop.

None of it did, of course. But there were others that offered all sorts of spiritual cures to what ailed him—everything from whacked-out do-it-yourself New Age stuff that seemed like witchcraft lite to weird earnest people telling him that Jesus was the only way.

He drove a few blocks west toward the bar near the college campus where his band had performed earlier that evening. There were a few people wandering the streets, but it was pretty quiet. He got out of his car and walked across the grassy quadrangle. Outside the student rec center, telephone poles were plastered with flyers advertising everything from apartments to poetry slams to beater vehicles. "Just another strip mall," he thought.

He saw a flyer advertising his band's show earlier that night and walked over to yank it off the pole.

When he did, he discovered an invitation with his name tattooed onto it.

Even when his piercing blue eyes looked straight at you, it was more like looking into a murky swamp than a clear pool.

Most days, after the first shift nurses cleaned him up, they'd prop him in his wheelchair and push him into the day room, where he'd spend the morning staring blankly at the TV. Lunch, more TV, dinner, more TV, bed.

Every once in a while, when his kids and grandkids came to visit, the staff used to notice that the water in the swamp settled a bit. Sometimes, there was a faint flicker of light that cut through the muddy shadow. But the last few times they'd come, he looked at them the same way he looked at the nursing home staff. He didn't recognize them anymore.

He had once run a successful insurance agency, been a husband and a devoted father who'd put three kids through parochial school and college and helped each one with a down payment on their first houses. He had served at church and in the community.

And now, his vacant eyes stared at the television or out the window or at a dust bunny waltzing across the floor.

Once a month, a few ragtag members of a church group would come to the Alzheimer's unit and sing a few hymns. Weeks after he'd stopped recognizing anyone, they were there for their monthly visit.

As a little boy he went to a small country church every Sunday. That's where he'd first heard that God had a son and his name was Jesus and that this Son was born to die for sinners just like him. The preacher prayed a prayer, and the little boy prayed right along with the preacher, asking Jesus to forgive all his sins and be his Savior.

The little boy opened his hymnal after he prayed that prayer. Inserted in the hymnal on the page for "Amazing Grace" was a simple, hand-lettered invitation, addressed to him. At the time, the event to which he'd been invited seemed far away, but he'd carried it with him his whole life, ready to respond. He'd lived his whole life saying "Yes, Lord." The invitation finally disappeared when his efficient daughter cleaned out his house before moving him into the nursing home.

The woman with the guitar began to sing:

Amazing grace! How sweet the sound!
That saved a wretch like me!

His cracked, rarely-used voice joined hers.

I once was lost, but now am found,
Was blind, but now I see.

For a few moments, he was completely present. As soon as the song ended, his eyes clouded over again. That was that.

But somewhere inside his soul, far beyond the decomposing neurotransmitters and physical decline, the words of the invitation were as clear as day.

"Come in, come in, Tina," Sharon said warmly to her visitor. "May I take your coat?"

Tina looked around the home. Cozy, comfortable, the living room had some warm furniture gathered in a conversation grouping. The home smelled of orange furniture polish and homemade bread.

"Won't you have a seat?" Sharon said, gesturing toward the loveseat. She settled in across from Tina and leaned forward expectantly.

Tina noticed the large, triple-matted, expensively framed invitation centered above the sofa behind her. "What a lovely invitation," she commented.

"Yes," Sharon said. "It's very special to us. We come from a long line of invitees, and it's been handed down from generation to generation. My children all know that this invitation is a part of our heritage. We go to church with other invited ones, take vacations with other invited families. We believe that this invitation sets boundaries around our lives and helps us live in blessing. We are good people, just the kind of people who really should be invited."

Tina sat there for a moment, stunned. She'd recently gotten an invitation to the same event. She could never have earned an invitation like that, or reciprocated in any way, so the generosity and kindness of it took her breath away. She had responded immediately. She looked across the room and saw the response card mounted in the frame, peeking out from the invitation attractively. Tina rose and looked closely at the aging invitation. "You were supposed to RSVP years ago, it says here."

"Respond? Why, we've lived as invited ones for years. Just look at our lifestyle," Sharon replied warmly. Tina didn't know what to say. Her eyes fell on the attractive grouping of family photos resting on top of an upright piano. "We've chosen to respond to the invitation from the comfort of our home. We have learned that we can have the goodness of the banquet delivered to us, right here!"

Tina was confused. Could she really stay right where she was and have the banquet delivered to her? Smiling, confident Sharon was telling her it was possible.

Tina looked again at the invitation and knew it wasn't.

In Real Time

If we're willing to live incarnationally, we'll discover that our days are saturated with God's invitations. Living incarnationally means that we seek to put flesh on the mystery of God-with-us, allowing his presence to shape our moments and days. As we do, we discover his invitations are tucked in the stack of dirty dishes piled next to the sink or jammed under the windshield wiper of our cars. The invitations may come in the form of a phone call from a friend (or an enemy!), a looming deadline on a test or project, sickness or grief, or beautiful sunsets or road construction.

His invitations are most definitely not historical documents or a piece of our proud religious heritage or even a past-tense prayer of commitment. Damaged, broken people often have eyes to see his invitations tucked into the cracks of their lives. Weary people discover his invitation when they're too tired to take another step. Little ones ... and old ones who are children again find his invitations scattered across their days like confetti.

So can you.

Jesus hides his invitation in plain sight. Look here:

Jesus resumed talking to the people, but now tenderly. "The Father has given me all these things to do and say. This is a unique Father-Son operation, coming out of Father and Son intimacies and knowledge. No one knows the Son the way the Father does, nor the Father the way the Son does. But I'm not keeping it to myself; I'm ready to go over it line by line with anyone willing to listen.

"Are you tired? Worn out? Burned out on religion? Come to me. Get away with me and you'll recover your life. I'll show you how to take a real rest. Walk with me and work with me—watch how I do it. Learn the unforced

rhythms of grace. I won't lay anything heavy or ill-fitting
on you. Keep company with me and you'll learn to live
freely and lightly."

(Mt 11:27–30 *The Message*)

In the days leading up to his crucifixion, Jesus told a slightly different form of the parable of the invited guests (Mt 22:1–14) to an audience of people who weren't just suspicious of him, but openly antagonistic. Matthew's version of the parable includes a sad commentary on Israel's history: God had sent prophets for generations to his people with the goal of bringing them back to him; mostly, their messages had fallen on hostile, unhearing ears. Matthew's recounting of the story also includes an image of a person who'd not only neglected to RSVP, but decided to crash the party with all the grace of a gang of thugs.

It's worth rereading both parables, prayerfully asking Jesus to show you the ways you've chosen to …

… stay at your own party.

… say you're going to attend his party, then stand him up.

… say yes.

Continue the Conversation:

What is the most surprising invitation you've ever received? What made it so?

CHAPTER THREE

Monochrome Rainbow

Living a Full-Spectrum Life

The Story of the Dirge that Rocked the House

> To what, then, can I compare the people of this generation? What are they like? They are like children sitting in the marketplace and calling out to each other: "We played the flute for you, and you did not dance; we sang a dirge, and you did not cry." For John the Baptist came neither eating bread nor drinking wine, and you say, "He has a demon." The Son of Man came eating and drinking, and you say, "Here is a glutton and a drunkard, a friend of tax collectors and 'sinners.'" But wisdom is proved right by all her children.
>
> —*LUKE 7:31–35*

To what can I compare this generation? They are like children sitting in the marketplaces and calling out to others: "We played the flute for you, and you did not dance; we sang a dirge and you did not mourn." For John came neither eating nor drinking, and they say, "He has a demon." The Son of Man came eating and drinking, and they say, "Here is a glutton and a drunkard, a friend of tax collectors and 'sinners.'" But wisdom is proved right by her actions.

—*Matthew 11:16–19*

Reloaded:
We Interrupt your Regularly Scheduled Program ...

Silence isn't always golden.

After 400 years of pregnant prophetic silence in Israel, a period of Israel's history filled with harsh rule by outsiders, moral decay, and occasional bursts of attempted spiritual renewal, you'd figure Israel would welcome the interruption in its regularly scheduled program.

The interruption came in the form of one John the Baptizer. John appeared in the echoing desert like a crack of thunder at high noon. He was the ancient equivalent of someone today who lives off the land in uninhabited Wyoming, sleeping in a lean-to and stitching together clothing from ragged bits of burlap while warming himself over a small ferocious fire. Out in the desert, John could feel the weight of God's lament for his screwed up, renegade people.

John couldn't do anything but belt out this lament at Volume 11. He summoned people moved by the cry to turn away from their sin and be immersed in a river to demonstrate their repentance. Some did. Lots of others just went to watch the show.

Luke's gospel as told in *The Message* tells what happened next: "When crowds of people came out for baptism because it was the popular thing to do, John exploded: 'Brood of snakes! What do you think you're doing slithering down here to the river? Do you think a little water on your snakeskins is going to deflect God's judgment? It's your life that must change, not your skin. And don't think you can pull rank by claiming Abraham as "father." Being a child of Abraham is neither here nor there—children of Abraham are a dime a dozen. God can make children from stones if he wants. What counts is your life. Is it green and blossoming? Because if it's deadwood, it goes on the fire'" (Lk 3:7–9).

John's radical message (and delivery) got people to wondering if he was The One, The Promise, The Messiah.

John's response to their curiosity? You people think I'm radical? Just wait.

They didn't have to wait long. When John's cousin Jesus came out to the desert asking John to baptize him, John took a stagger-step backwards, shaking his head in shock at the request.

"No," John whispered. "Not you. You have nothing to repent of. I can't." Time stopped for a moment as the two men stood in the hot sun, staring one another down. John had known Jesus his entire life. He'd always known that Jesus was different from everyone else, just like he'd always known he was a little out of sync with the rest of the kids. But what John saw and felt in that single moment in the desert, looking into Jesus's eyes caused him to ask, simply, "Why are you coming to me? I need to be baptized by *you*."

Jesus told him that this was how it needed to be: "Do it. God's work, putting things right, begins here in my baptism." John agreed, and both men stepped into the water.

After his baptism, Jesus showed the effect this act had on his life by traveling around the area like a drifter, going to parties, hanging around with the wrong crowd and breaking rules. Meanwhile, John was living out there in the desert singing a dirge with the lyrics "repent, repent, repent." He told people to get ready for God's coming revolution by doing a 180 in their lives, turning to God full-on, and jettisoning the clutter holding them back from running toward him. John was asking people to ready themselves for ... Jesus? The people were supposed to repent so they could party with Jesus?

It wasn't long before John was tossed in jail for disturbing the peace of the government authorities. John had always been completely convinced of his message, but in the silence of his prison cell, he wondered if his certainty was misplaced. He'd cried a single-note, minor key lament for the entire time he lived out in the wild. Jesus was now living a song of celebration that harmonized with that lament in a way that John could never have dreamed. Not all those nights sleeping under God's stars in the desert. Not now in the restless dark of the graybar motel.

So John sent a message to his cousin and friend, Jesus, asking if he really was the one for whom John had been paving the way. John knew ... he'd probably always known. His humble response to Jesus's request for baptism shows that he knew that Jesus had nothing of which to repent, and that Jesus was different from the rest of the crowd who'd trekked out to the desert.

But there in the darkness, facing death, John needed to know one more time.

Jesus gave an answer to the messengers bearing John's query, explaining what was happening as he traveled around the area, going to parties, hanging around with the wrong crowd, and breaking rules. "Go back and report to John what you hear and see: The blind receive sight, the lame walk, those who have leprosy are cured, the deaf hear, the dead are raised, and the good news is preached to the poor. Blessed is the man who does not fall away on account of me" (Mt 11: 4–6).

In effect, he said, "Yeah, John. This is exactly what you were preparing them for. This is it ... the promise, the revolution, the kingdom. It's me. Don't cave now."

The crowd following Jesus hears his message to John and watches his eyes follow the departing messengers who carry his heart back to John. When he turns his attention back to the crowd, his words are blade sharp love.

He compares them to too-cool junior high boys who've been invited to attend a funeral for a younger classmate's hamster or a concert of oldies music with their hopelessly old parents. No matter what the event, these kids sit slouched on their couches, arms folded, full of criticism: "Stupid little kids have funerals for rodents." "The parents' geezer music is so lame." They're convinced there is something horribly wrong with these activities, with the people who'd dare to ask them to participate, and probably with the entire world in general.

Jesus's audience was just like those oppositional young adolescents: The dirge of John's message in the desert? Too harsh, they said. The joyful party music of Jesus? Too libertine, they said.

His audience had mentally crossed their arms, slouched down in their chairs, and turned down the music.

Jesus doesn't leave the meaning of this parable shrouded in mystery for his hearers as he did with so many of his other stories. He tells them that their oh-so-genius analysis of John's message and his own may not be all that brilliant. Though the wording of Jesus's pointed conclusion varies slightly in Luke and Matthew's recounting of this story: "But wisdom is proved right by all her children" (Lk 7:35).; "But wisdom is proved right by her actions" (Mt 11:19).; the meaning doesn't vary one centimeter.

You're not wise and mature if you sit slouched in a chair, criticizing and putting your fingers in your ears to silence the song John and I are singing, Jesus told them. Respond to the song by dancing to it with your life, and you'll understand the meaning of this profound, eternal music.

ParableLife: Bucket of Black

"Dude, my church isn't anything like the church you grew up in," Josh said. "I don't blame you for being gun-shy. But it really is different. God used it to change my life."

"I've heard that one before," Eric replied. "It's the marketing tag on every other church out there. They say, 'We're not church as usual.' It's all hype." Eric stared out the greasy window of the Gold Coin. When was the last time the health department stopped by this place? If cleanliness was any clue, he guessed it had been quite a while. The food was fast and cheap, and the proprietor didn't mind if people sat there for hours living their lives. How the place ever turned a profit when it seemed the only thing guys like him ordered were Velveeta-drenched French fries and coffee was beyond him.

The Gold Coin was the safest place Eric knew. In a lot of ways, it was like a church—a sanctuary, a community, someplace that fed body and soul. The food he dumped into his body may not have been all that healthy, but at least it didn't leave him feeling shamed and hollow like church did.

"No thanks," he repeated. He stubbed out his cigarette and swiped at the bill Yolanda had left on the table. "Maybe some other time." Like when they serve Haagen-Dazs in hell.

Josh smiled and grabbed the bill out of his hand. "No time like the present, man. You've told me that you don't usually hit the clubs on Saturdays 'til after ten. So I'll pick you up about six and you can come to the Saturday night service. We can do church, then grab some dinner somewhere where they use real ingredients." He grinned, picked a single cold cheese fry off Eric's plate, and rose to leave.

Eric wandered into the colorless wet cold of the early March day. How did that just happen? Church? Saturday? He swore under his breath. Gray slush squooshed around his orange Chuck Taylors as he trudged up the street back to work. Gunmetal sky, salt-frosted vehicles—the monochromatic color scheme was the exact image Eric had of his childhood religious experience.

Josh meant well, but no way was he gonna drag Eric back to any of it.

Everything inside of him screamed for color and life. The Jesus Eric knew when he was a kid kept all 64 Crayolas locked safely away in heaven. Color and joy were a heavenly reward, not an earthly pleasure. Kingdom come, Eric, they'd told him. Here on earth, you work, you keep your nose clean, you marry and have 2.4 kids, a dog ... you stay planted. You think you're too good for this place, you gotta go somewhere else? God and everything else you need to live life is here, they told him.

The colors and textures of life drew Eric toward a design career, over his stern parents' objections. They had the same emotional tenor as the couple in *American Gothic*, but with less of a sense of humor. Everyone back in his northern Wisconsin hometown did. It was a gritty, silent place, populated by "us" and "them," his parents' distinction for those who attended church versus those who didn't except maybe on Christmas and Easter. The few, the chosen, the elect—the group to which Eric's family belonged—were pitted in this cosmic combat against the good ol' boys in their plaid shirts and mesh caps who lived at the bar when they weren't working at the mill. His parents told him his job as one of the few, the chosen, the elect was to stay unpolluted by the world and all of its colors and textures. Their response to Eric's dreams: "Why do you need a stupid fairy career like art when you can have a nice secure job at the bank as head teller?"

When Eric packed his bags and left home at nineteen, he never looked back except in mocking anger. The religion of his parents could be boiled down to just one word: NO. He told God goodbye and good riddance, and left him behind in his hometown.

The ten years since he left northern Wisconsin had been filled with a riot of primal color. Eric worked his way through design school, while committing himself to experiencing the big bad world that frightened his parents so. He kept dumping chunks of brightly hued paint pigment into his life so he could saturate his canvas-blank soul: clubbing, a lot of sexual experimentation, a couple of failed relationships, a regular intake of drugs and alcohol.

Every first-year art student knows that when you mix all the paint pigments, you get a bucket of black.

His quest for experiencing all the colors of city life had cost him his first two jobs after college, but he'd landed on his feet when he'd gotten a job with a small design house with a laid-back vibe right in his neighborhood. That's where he met Josh, a vendor for a paper supplier. They discovered they shared the same taste in movies and music, and Eric really liked Josh's quick wit. When Josh stopped by the design studio on his regular sales call, they'd walk up the block to the Gold Coin and grab lunch.

It didn't take long before God kept popping up in their conversations. Eric liked Josh, but squirmed inside when The Name came up. He'd shut down, stare through the film of grease on the windows, and wait for the storm of spiritual words to pass: "God answered my prayer about my roommate situation. This week at church, God was moving. It was really powerful … Jesus completely changed my life … ."

Josh, it seemed, belonged to a church full of drama and music and emotion. He was determined to drag Eric there with him. Josh cheerfully ignored Eric's non-responsiveness, and kept salting their conversations with references to the subject.

Eric liked Josh, really he did, but he couldn't listen to the God talk splashing into the conversation any more. Eric broke his silence at lunch that day, telling Josh about what it was like to grow up with sunglasses forced onto his face, every color filtered to gray. He went through a half a pack of cigarettes telling his story while Josh listened quietly. Then, depleted, he stubbed out his smoke and looked Josh in the eye. "Glad it's working for you. But I've been there, done that."

Eric figured that would be the final word. But when Josh picked up the check at lunch, he said, "I'm not trying to sell you on Jesus. You pride yourself on being open-minded, right? Well, it sounds like you've had the trial and convicted the entire Christian world just on the basis of one place that hurt you. That colorlessness? It's not God."

The next thing he knew, Josh told him he'd stop by to pick him up about six on Saturday night. And then he was gone.

Josh was right about at least one thing, Eric thought, as he slouched in his chair during the service. The church *was* different from the gray, dreary church of Eric's childhood. It had decent artwork painted onto the walls of the old auto body shop they used for a meeting place, a band playing coffeebar worship music, a pastor whose message seemed more like a conversation between friends, and a bunch of people who didn't seem afraid to feel. They all appear completely convinced that God was in the house and that he was speaking. They were all doing their darndest to listen.

Eric thought the whole thing felt surreal, like someone had overlaid the transparent neon colors of a rave over his childhood religious experience. After the final song, Josh introduced Eric to some of his friends, and a bunch of them grabbed Thai food at a place near the church. Josh joked about the lack of fast food on the menu and was careful not to ask Eric what he thought about the church service. After dinner, he dropped Eric off at his apartment as promised and simply said, "Thanks for coming, man."

Eric shrugged and walked back into his apartment.

As he sat alone smoking in the dark, Eric felt a stifling anger drape him like a heavy woolen blanket. He was angry at the years of colorless northern Wisconsin traditional religion given him by his harsh, cold parents. He'd run from it all ten years ago looking for color, and was angry that in the end all he'd found was a darker shade of the same empty gray he'd grown up with. Both extremes were nothing more than shades of black.

He thought about walking up to the Gold Coin, but he didn't have the energy to get out of his chair. He lit another cigarette and watched the smoke drift away from him.

It occurred to Eric that what he really wanted was to be a child standing in the sunlight, bathed in the prismed colors of a rainbow. He ran his hand through his hair, then raised it for just a moment like he'd seen the desperate praying, worshiping people do tonight at Josh's church. Reaching.

A splinter of light echoed off the edge of a picture frame. He stretched his hand toward it for a flash of a second, the gesture a wordless prayer.

God heard him loud and clear.

In Real Time

Some people love the challenge of acquiring data and possessing knowledge. For these people, knowledge is a bookshelf stocked with a lovely set of matching encyclopedias. Lots of other people are happy to borrow someone else's knowledge, acquiring it secondhand, so they don't have to wrestle through a subject for themselves. When this happens, knowledge can sometimes become a steaming pile of clichés.

Jesus told those who tried to find a way to fit him onto their bookshelf with the rest of the data—and those who listened to him while crouching behind a mound of clichés—that their lives have all the impact of judges at a county fair dog show. Jesus told his knowledge-proud, wisdom-poor hearers the story about the children on the playground so that they could become children who could dance in joyful obedience to heaven's music, following his lead.

Saul, a guy who ran his life using a set of knowledge encyclopedias while sitting on a metaphorical pile of religious clichés, was transformed by a radical encounter with the risen Christ. Saul became Paul, Christ's passionate follower. Saul/Paul's pious encyclopedia set and cliché pile were both incinerated by the fire of his encounter. Some of it became ash, nothing more than useless byproduct of Paul's former life.

Other parts of Paul's religious knowledge transformed into wisdom. Christ's death on the cross breathed life into the God-knowledge that Saul had accumulated. Paul described the transformation of knowledge into wisdom like this:

For the message of the cross
is foolishness to those who are perishing,
but to us who are being saved it is the power of God.
For it is written:
"I will destroy the wisdom of the wise;
the intelligence of the intelligent I will frustrate."

Where is the wise man? Where is the scholar?
Where is the philosopher of this age?
Has not God made foolish the wisdom of the world?
For since in the wisdom of God
the world through its wisdom did not know him,
God was pleased through the foolishness
of what was preached to save those who believe.
Jews demand miraculous signs
and Greeks look for wisdom,
but we preach Christ crucified:
a stumbling block to Jews and foolishness to Gentiles,
but to those whom God has called, both Jews and Greeks,
Christ the power of God and the wisdom of God.
For the foolishness of God is wiser than man's wisdom,
and the weakness of God is stronger than man's strength.

Brothers, think of what you were when you were called.
Not many of you were wise by human standards;
not many were influential; not many were of noble birth.
But God chose the foolish things of the world
to shame the wise;
God chose the weak things of the world to shame the strong.
He chose the lowly things of this world
and the despised things—and the things that are not—
to nullify the things that are,
so that no one may boast before him.
It is because of him that you are in Christ Jesus,
who has become for us wisdom from God—that is, our
righteousness, holiness and redemption.
Therefore, as it is written:
"Let him who boasts boast in the Lord."

(1 Cor 1:18–31)

Paul's transformation made him willing to dive into the mystery about which he wrote so eloquently: Every character trait of God, every rule, every ordinance, everything we could know about him was contained in the flesh and blood of the man Christ Jesus. Paul knew that the boy Jesus had once hammered nails with his earthly dad. Paul knew that Jesus the adult had touched untouchables and called them his friends. He healed. He delivered. In the end, Jesus was hammered onto a cross.

Paul spent the rest of his life following the risen Christ. He proclaimed confidently that Jesus was God's wisdom in the flesh, calling each one of us to become his children so that we can dance on the playground to the music of heaven.

Jesus calls us to follow him away from the earthbound knowledge that creates extreme legalism and sophisticated license. It may be that you can hear the call loudest in a place of silence. If you can find a place of intentional solitude (a park, a trail, even the quiet of your home with all the media switched off) to quiet yourself and listen, you may be amazed at what you hear. Take some time to ponder each phrase of Paul's words from 1 Corinthians. Listen closely, and you may begin to hear each beat of the dirge and the celebration in his words. He isn't calling you to another extreme. He is calling you to a radical rhythm of obedience that looks a lot like wisdom.

Continue the Conversation:
Describe the most extreme person you know. What makes him or her so? What do you most admire about this person? What do you fear most about the extremes he or she represents?

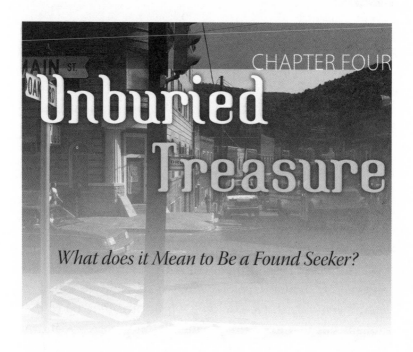

CHAPTER FOUR

Unburied Treasure

What does it Mean to Be a Found Seeker?

Found Valuables

> The kingdom of heaven is like treasure hidden in a field.
> When a man found it, he hid it again, and then in his joy
> went and sold all he had and bought that field.
>
> Again, the kingdom of heaven is like a merchant
> looking for fine pearls. When he found one of great value,
> he went away and sold everything he had and bought it.
>
> —*Matthew 13:44–46*

Reloaded: Slide Show

Reading these two brief parables is like watching a slide show.
The first slide in the series is a vivid photo of the stunned,
joyous face of someone who has stumbled on a treasure
worth more than everything he currently owns. This slide

is followed by one showing him patting dirt over the spot where he's reburied it. He's looking over his left shoulder, making sure no one sees him at work.

The next slide is him packing all of his beat-up stuff into a first century version of a U-Haul. And then: a shot of him selling the entire contents of the U-Haul at a flea market. He wears a poker face, blank as an empty billboard, in the slide that shows him handing the money to a landowner and receiving a deed to the piece of property where he'd carefully reburied the treasure for safekeeping. The last in the series is a near-duplicate of the first: a joyous face cradling the treasure that he's traded all to possess.

A couple of black slides signal a transition. They're followed by a new face—a young man apprenticed to a veteran gemologist. He's holding a precious stone up to the sunlight, his mentor waiting patiently for an assessment. A few more slides of the two of them working together follow the first slide. The young man in the first slide seems to age and mature in each successive photo as his mentor fades into the background.

Finally, he's on his own—the next slide shows him haggling with another merchant over a handful of second-quality pearls. A quick succession of shots follows him as he plies his trade in cities across the Middle East. Expensive clothing reflects his growing success.

His success story is interrupted by a shot of a single, perfect pearl lying on a piece of deep purple fabric. Even the untrained eye can see its beauty. The next slide is a photo of our businessman's eyes, and the angle of the camera catches the reflection of the pearl in his pupil.

From this point forward the arc of the gemologist's story is a carbon copy of the treasure-finder's. That day, Jewel Man sells his entire inventory. The slide show ends with a picture of him standing alone at the edge of a desert, his hand open to the white sunlight. In his hand is a pure, perfect moon, his pearl, reflecting the sun. Everything he ever learned about precious gems has been nothing more than a prelude to this moment.

The image stays frozen on the screen.

Jesus tells these parables at the height of his popularity, and the word pictures are as vivid to his hearers as visual images are to us. The crowds grabbed at him, loving what they'd seen he could do for them—healing some of them, setting others free from demonic oppression. They loved how he could silence the always-talking teachers who'd been all too willing to tell the rest of them how to live.

The crowd is ready to listen to anything he has to say. They think they're ready to do whatever he suggests.

But he doesn't suggest anything to them. Instead, he speaks in parable. You can find seven of these stories in Matthew 13 including the two detailed here. The simplicity of these two little bursts of story veils the difficult truth Jesus speaks.

How difficult? Most in the crowd couldn't imagine trading away everything they held dear in order to find their home in an invisible kingdom. How difficult? It's as incomprehensible for us today as it was for Jesus's first century followers. In our culture of shattered promises and litigious hair-splitting, committing everything to gain One Thing terrifies most of us.

Which is why Jesus had to do it first.

He allowed himself to be torn from his Father to find you. If you bear his name, you have been given a new identity as a treasure finder, a pearl hunter. It's not a hobby or a part-time

job or even a smart career move. Learning to live as a seeker
only happens once we truly realize that we've been found.

The next slide in the story?

You.

ParableLife: Bombardment

All of my life, I've felt like a displaced person. It wasn't
because we moved around a lot. My family relocated once,
when I was thirteen, to a home about fifteen minutes away
from where I'd spent my elementary school years. It wasn't
because there were disrupted relationships at the core of my
life. There weren't.

However, home didn't always feel like a safe place. The
only other place that might have served as a refuge during
my childhood should have been school, but Mr. Slovowsky's
gym class and the team games on the playground amped
homeless feelings in my soul.

This is because I was a smart, bookish nerd-girl who was
always the second-to-last one picked for all team sports.
As an adult, I'm amazed at how many people I meet who
say they were the last ones picked in gym class while they
were growing up. There are many of us who've suffered the
indignity of waiting for someone to tell us we could be on
their team.

That eternal wait of watching everyone except Ellen
Friedman get chosen before me for every team ever assembled
at Mark Twain Elementary School telegraphed me a loud,
painful message: Hey Loser! You don't belong!

Mr. Slovowsky, the sadistic gym teacher of my childhood
nightmares, didn't do much to help the situation. Even his
name—Slovowsky—conjures the figure of a tattooed drill

sergeant making scrawny recruits do one-armed pushups to the 1960s song "Go You Chicken Fat, Go" in the pouring rain, a twisted grin on his war-scarred face.

It would probably be fair to mention at this point that my childhood memories might not be entirely accurate. Hindsight and life experience tell me today that Mr. Slovowsky just may have been an aging former jock who ended up with a Phys Ed teaching gig by default, not desire.

One thing was certain—Mr. Slovowsky wasn't much for lesson planning. It seemed like we spent at least three or four solid months each year in P.E. doing nothing but playing Bombardment. Bombardment, also known as Dodgeball, seemed to define my place in the world.

The Mark Twain Elementary School version of Bombardment wasn't the formal affair depicted in the scatological 2004 Ben Stiller movie *Dodgeball*. Instead, our low-tech, high-torture version would begin when Mr. Slovowsky would pick his two pets to be team captains and let them loose on the rest of us. For me, it meant sitting on the dusty gym floor and waiting … and waiting … and waiting until someone was forced to pick me.

Draft accomplished, Slovowsky would send each team to one end of the gym and tell us to face the other team, each side lined up like a firing squad. Which, of course, was exactly what we were.

Mr. Slovowsky then proceeded to toss a few hard red rubber playground balls into the middle of the gym and blow his whistle, signaling that the carnage could begin. He'd settle his middle-aged girth on a rusting metal folding chair and watch dispassionately as the brave kids ran out, grabbed the balls that rolled onto their side of the gym, and then whipped the balls as hard as they could at the kids who were lined up against the opposite wall.

If you got hit by one of those red rubber missiles, you had to go and sit on the floor next to Mr. Slovowsky's folding chair. The idea was that the weak would be quickly picked off and the strong would survive. It seemed like someone had to go to the nurse about once a week because he had a bloody nose or a broken wrist from all this physical education. I read not long ago that many school districts have banned this game, for obvious reasons.

But back in Mr. Slovowsky's day, we were all trapped in that gym. There was no school district trying to protect us from the terrors of Bombardment. There was just Mr. Slovowsky and his chair and his whistle.

Oddly enough, I always ended up as one of the last standing on the firing line. It wasn't because of my natural grace and athleticism. It was because I hated pain. I hated the angry red welt that came along with getting whacked with one of those rock-hard playground balls. So I learned to hide behind the kids who cannoned those balls as if their lives depended on it, probably because in some weird way, their lives did.

A lot of kids seemed to thrive on this sort of testosterone-based competition. My aversion to Bombardment ended up making me oddly successful at it. My strategy was to try to tuck myself in a corner. If that didn't work, I'd run klutzily from one spot along the wall to another, hiding behind the kids who were actually firing those balls at each other. When there were no more kids to hide behind, I ended up getting clobbered. Hard.

Bombardment summed up for me the way the world seemed to work. The strong and wily survive; the klutzy, the homely, the Losers get clobbered and have to sit on the filthy gym floor next to Mr. Slovowsky's rusty metal chair, watching.

Pretty much all of my life had the feel of a Bombardment game that went on 24/7. As I approached adolescence, I figured out, like many teens do, how to dig a bunker for myself and try to find a safe place to hide from the rest of the Bombardment-playing world. I constructed my hiding place out of reefer and promiscuity and alcohol. It didn't take me too long to figure out that my hiding place wasn't any safer than the outside world. I'd Bombarded myself.

When a friend started visiting me in my self-constructed bunker and talking to me about Jesus, I thought she was whacked. It seems that she'd just "become a Christian," whatever that meant. In my secular Jewish head, if a person wasn't Jewish by heritage, then they were probably Christians unless their family came from some distant corner of the globe. I believed that most Americans were Christians.

She encouraged me to read the Bible, which seemed patently absurd to me. Everyone knew the Bible was a nothing more than a disorganized but moderately interesting classic book of fiction.

She kept telling me that her book wasn't fiction, but Truth. Even weirder, she insisted that I needed to check out the New Testament. Why on earth would a secular Jewish girl like me touch that Gentile book?

It wasn't her compelling theology that made her words begin to soften my Bombardment-weary heart. Nor was it her skillful apologetic defense of her faith, because, mostly, she just talked about whatever she was reading in the Bible with me. She didn't freak out when I asked questions or said strange things. Her radically changed life wasn't much of a heart-softener for me, either. For a span of time after she "became a Christian," she continued to join me in my emotional bunker and smoke weed while we talked about God. (This particular evangelism technique certainly wouldn't be taught in any Sunday School class, that's for sure.)

I wrestled my way through much of the Old Testament, which was somewhat more familiar to me, during those months. I didn't understand a whole lot of what I was reading, but there was a love and a power that made the words seem to jump off the pages. It was like the author of those words was there, speaking them to me. Me! The klutz. The loser. The one who didn't believe. The second-to-the-last-to-be-picked-for-Bombardment.

Why would he do that?

When I cried out, weary from no small amount of spiritual pain, asking God to explain why a not-so-nice Jewish girl like me needed to come to terms with who Jesus was and is, he found me, cowering in my bunker of substance abuse, promiscuity, and despair.

He had every right to pelt me with lots and lots of angry red playground balls. Instead, he held me close enough so that I could hear his heart beating. He wanted to love me and show me what his Father was like.

"Try reading the gospel of John," my friend patiently encouraged. "The answers to your questions are there."

When I did, I was stunned at Jesus's words about himself: "I am the way and the truth and the life. No one comes to the Father except through me. If you really knew me, you would know my Father as well. From now on, you do know him and have seen him" (Jn 14:6).

In that moment of eternal clarity, his arms around me, I was safe for the first time in my life.

And when I looked closely at those arms, I saw them covered with angry red welts in the shape of those terrible playground balls.

While recovering from opium addiction during the late 1800s, struggling believer and poet Francis Thompson penned these words in his most famous work, "The Hound Of Heaven":

> *I fled Him, down the nights and down the days;*
> *I fled Him, down the arches of the years;*
> *I fled Him, down the labyrinthine ways*
> *Of my own mind; and in the midst of tears*
> *I hid from Him, and under running laughter.*
> *Up vistaed hopes I sped;*
> *And shot, precipitated,*
> *Adown Titanic glooms of chasmed fears,*
> *From those strong Feet that followed, followed after.*
> *But with unhurrying chase,*
> *And unperturbed pace,*
> *Deliberate speed, majestic instancy,*
> *They beat—and a Voice beat*
> *More instant than the Feet—*
> *'All things betray thee, who betrayest Me.'*

There are many of us who run, looking for a place to hide, hoping we won't be discovered or hurt. Like the pearl merchant in the parable, "with unhurrying chase and unperturbed pace, deliberate speed, majestic instancy" Jesus searches out each one of us in our hiding places. He is completely certain that you are the most beautiful pearl there is, and he sacrificed everything to have you.

My foolish response to God's amazing love was to learn, at last, to play Bombardment. I learned how from the church.

The first three years after I came to faith in Christ, I continued to camp out in my bunker, though now I did it without anesthesia. My parents were glad to have a functional child in the house again, but, understandably, were just-this-side of furious when I told them that I believed in Jesus. Christianity and anti-Semitism were like cojoined twins in their minds, as they are in the minds of many Jews. Those feelings are painfully, and yet sadly, understandable given history's facts.

I was forbidden to attend church while I still lived at home. For three years after I began following Jesus, I had church in my room, reading my Bible, praying, writing, and listening to a Christian radio station (Bless you, WMBI!). I hung out with some of the other Christian kids at school, and I'd occasionally sneak to a church service or a Bible study when I thought I could get away with it.

Those years gave me plenty of time to dream about what it would be like to be part of the church. Yeah, I understood that I already was part of the church ... but I longed to be on a team. I filtered everything I read in my Bible about church through that longing. I imagined that the church was a family, happy and functional, and that people would greet each other with stories about the amazing things God had done in their lives that day. I'd mentally zapped past the New Testament words that detailed conflict and sin, selfishness and confusion.

When I headed off to college, I dove head-first into the world of church. Bible study? I was there. Church service? Ditto. Fellowship groups, prayer groups ... I tried a whole lot of everything.

Along the way, I've met some amazing people who were head-over-heels in love with Jesus, their Rescuer and Lord. At the same time, I've seen behavior in others that had an eerie similarity to the mean-spirited climate of Mr. Slovowsky's gym class: Favoritism, nepotism, financial misdealings, sexual abuse and addiction, angry legalism, anything-goes-licentiousness, and a desperate need among many leaders (team captains) to control and win.

I'm sad to tell you that I became a student of the game. There were so many willing, friendly Bombardment instructors in the churches I attended.

I'd love to report that I saw the game for what it was—a non-Biblical version of what we believers were supposed to be—Christ's hands and feet and heart, inviting others to know and be known by him. I wish I could tell you I refused to play the game. I saw it for what it was early on, that's true. But there was an unhealed place in me that longed to not only be on the team, but maybe even to be a captain once in a while.

I never got very good at Bombardment, even with all the coaching. I know now that this was God's mercy in my life. I have been on the receiving end of some stinging red missiles that have left me crumpled on the ground. Church politics backfired. Betrayed by people I thought were friends. Gossip. Gamesmanship. Angry playground balls, flung deliberately. And precisely.

The last time this happened, I laid flat on my face, writhing in pain and wondered what the point of this stupid game was really supposed to be. My teammates had turned out to be not teammates at all, but professional opponents.

Out of the corner of my eye, I saw feet and hands. Pierced, bloody feet and hands, reaching for me. Again. Treasure, when I wasn't looking for him.

Poet Francis Thompson knew a thing or two about searching and being found:

> *(He said), 'And human love needs human meriting:*
> *How hast thou merited—*
> *Of all man's clotted clay the dingiest clot?*
> *Alack, thou knowest not*
> *How little worthy of any love thou art!*
> *Whom wilt thou find to love ignoble thee,*
> *Save Me, save only Me?*
> *All which I took from thee I did but take,*
> *Not for thy harms,*
> *But just that thou might'st seek it in My arms.*
> *All which thy child's mistake*
> *Fancies as lost, I have stored for thee at home:*
> *Rise, clasp My hand, and come!'*
> *Halts by me that footfall:*
> *Is my gloom, after all,*
> *Shade of His hand, outstretched caressingly?*
> *Ah, fondest, blindest, weakest,*
> *I am He Whom thou seekest!*
> *Thou drivest love from thee, who drivest Me.'*

The "Hound of Heaven" that Thompson discovered as a broken addict is the same one I found sprawled across the Bombardment court of the church. All of those church games left me depleted and empty. There are too many of us who live as though these games have huge consequence. Jesus didn't go to the trouble of finding us just so he could put us on teams and have us compete against one another for a here and now prize.

He calls us to live as a community of treasure seekers. A humbled posture—depleted, empty, and face to the ground—is the only certain way to find the treasure that matters: Him.

In Real Time

The two primary places I've experienced Bombardment were at school and in the church. Each of us has experienced the terrors of Bombardment somewhere in our lives—at work, in our families, among friends, or even within ourselves.

King David, who lived about 1,000 years before Christ, spent years of his life on the run, looking for a place to hide from enemies who wanted him eradicated. It was Extreme Bombardment.

At the height of this miserable experience, David wrote Psalm 27:

The Lord is my light and my salvation—whom shall I fear?
The Lord is the stronghold of my life—
of whom shall I be afraid?
When evil men advance against me to devour my flesh,
when my enemies and my foes attack me,
they will stumble and fall.
Though an army besiege me, my heart will not fear;
though war break out against me,
even then will I be confident.
One thing I ask of the Lord, this is what I seek:
that I may dwell in the house of the Lord
all the days of my life,
to gaze upon the beauty of the Lord
and to seek him in his temple.

For in the day of trouble he will keep me safe in his dwelling;
he will hide me in the shelter of his tabernacle
and set me high upon a rock.
Then my head will be exalted above
the enemies who surround me;
at his tabernacle will I sacrifice with shouts of joy;
I will sing and make music to the Lord.
Hear my voice when I call, O Lord;
be merciful to me and answer me.
My heart says of you, "Seek his face!"
Your face, Lord, I will seek.
Do not hide your face from me,
do not turn your servant away in anger;
you have been my helper.
Do not reject me or forsake me, O God my Savior.
Though my father and mother forsake me,
the Lord will receive me.
Teach me your way, O Lord;
lead me in a straight path because of my oppressors.
Do not turn me over to the desire of my foes,
for false witnesses rise up against me, breathing out violence.
I am still confident of this:
I will see the goodness of the Lord in the land of the living.
Wait for the Lord;
be strong and take heart and wait for the Lord.

In spite of the Death Bombardment Squads who'd driven him into bunkered caves in the desert, David found treasure there. The songs he wrote from that place in his life still resonate with truth today. Psalm 27 is a song for those who've been found, and for those who seek.

One powerful way to discover the truth-treasure that David found is by paraphrasing each phrase of this psalm. If you keep a journal, take some time today—or even better yet, over the next few days—to put each phrase into your own words. As you do, pray those phrases back to God.

Ask him to open your ears to hear his take on the effects that unhealthy competition has had in your life. Ask him to give you fresh vision to see the "treasures" (stuff, security, relationships, power) that you may be investing in so that you'll have a material edge.

David discovered his exit from Bombardment in the damp darkness of a cave. Jesus offers you and me the same kind of radical exit from the game when we choose to live "obsessed" with one thing—to find and be found by him.

Continue the Conversation:
Contemporary culture offers some powerful images of what a seeker is. What do you think of when you hear the word "seeker"? How do those images jive with the biblical image presented in the parables of the found treasure and pearl?

CHAPTER FIVE

Blind Justice

The Power of the Choice to Forgive

A Vigilante "Victim"

Then Peter came to Jesus and asked, "Lord, how many times shall I forgive my brother when he sins against me? Up to seven times?"

Jesus answered, "I tell you, not seven times, but seventy times seven. Therefore, the kingdom of heaven is like a king who wanted to settle accounts with his servants. As he began the settlement, a man who owed him ten thousand talents was brought to him. Since he was not able to pay, the master ordered that he and his wife and his children and all that he had be sold to repay the debt.

"The servant fell on his knees before him. 'Be patient with me,' he begged, 'and I will pay back everything.' The servant's master took pity on him, canceled the debt and let him go.

"But when that servant went out, he found one of his fellow servants who owed him a hundred denarii. He grabbed him and began to choke him. 'Pay back what you owe me!' he demanded.

"His fellow servant fell to his knees and begged him, 'Be patient with me, and I will pay you back.'

"But he refused. Instead, he went off and had the man thrown into prison until he could pay the debt. When the other servants saw what had happened, they were greatly distressed and went and told their master everything that had happened.

"Then the master called the servant in. 'You wicked servant,' he said, 'I canceled all that debt of yours because you begged me to. Shouldn't you have had mercy on your fellow servant just as I had on you?' In anger his master turned him over to the jailers to be tortured, until he should pay back all he owed.

"This is how my heavenly Father will treat each of you unless you forgive your brother from your heart."

—*Matthew 18:21–35*

Reloaded: Smooth Hands

I wonder if Eliud sat looking at his hands in the fading light his first night in prison. His hands were the unsoiled, smooth hands of someone who'd spent his life negotiating deals and pushing paperwork, not doing manual labor.

Eliud's hands had perhaps offered the Near East equivalent of a handshake on the agreement he'd struck with the king some time earlier. He'd borrowed enough money from the king to fund his latest building project—constructing the ancient equivalent of Trump Tower in downtown Jerusalem. "Yeah, king ... I'll even name the building after you," he gushed. "This is the investment of a lifetime. Once we're open for business, I'll be able to repay you easily. The money will roll in the front doors. It's a sure thing."

The king, who'd heard a sales pitch or two in his life, examined Eliud's track record. He was a sharp businessman with a decent credit history. But this project was ten times the size of anything he or anyone else in the kingdom had ever done. The king asked him what sort of collateral he was willing to offer.

"I'd bet my life, my family, all that I have. It's a sure thing, I tell you."

Eliud's rock-solid certainty began to dissolve into rubble as one problem after another plagued the project. He had troubles with suppliers. There were weather delays. A couple of the guys had accidents at the building site. He played one set of subcontractors off the other, loaning money to some of them in order to keep them on the job. He bounced checks to others. The whole project turned to a mountain of loose ends until finally all work on the structure ground to a halt.

The half-finished building hadn't been touched for over a year. The failure was more than he could face—he'd lost his "sure thing" gamble. But Eliud was unable to see himself as a loser. He hadn't gotten to where he was in life by thinking of himself as anything other than a shrewd businessman, and he was convinced that the project's failure was everyone else's fault.

He was almost able to forget about the truth—that he'd borrowed a boatload of money from the king—and he was responsible for repayment. He busied himself with the rest of his life, taking his wife out to dinner, going to his children's soccer games and ballet recitals.

Until the day he got the summons to appear before the king and repay the loan.

Eliud's route to see the king that day took him past the half-finished hulk of a building. He'd carefully avoided it for months. That day, he forced himself to go look at it, wishing that the building had magically constructed itself and this was all a bad dream. Nope. It was as unfinished as it had been the last time he'd been at the site. Excuses circled in his head like vultures as he walked toward the king's home.

The king smiled in greeting. Unbeknownst to Eliud, he had given him some extra time on the loan, injecting a dose of mercy into the process. The king had occasionally visited the building site, genuinely hoping that Eliud would be able to get the project moving again.

But the king couldn't wait forever. He knew that one day, maybe not so far in the future, the responsibility of running the kingdom would be handed down to his beloved son. The king wanted to make sure that all was in order before that time came. And this loan was a huge piece of unfinished business on the books.

The king extended his hand to the man. Eliud looked at him and threw himself onto the ground, prostrating himself; his unsoiled, smooth businessman's hands extended toward the king, begging for just a little more time. He was painfully aware of what he'd bartered for this loan. He and his family were going to spend the rest of their lives in slavery working off the debt if he couldn't figure out a way to repay it. He pleaded for more time, excuses spilling from his lips.

But when he looked up at the king, he could see that the king had already made his mind up about what his punishment was going to be. He said quietly, "I'm going wipe the debt off the records. It's gone as of this moment."

Eliud departed from the king's home that day certain of only one thing—that he was indeed innocent of any wrongdoing in the whole affair. His hands were clean.

Later that day, he ran into one of his subcontractors to whom he'd loaned a C-note a few months earlier. The sub—the low-life!—hadn't repaid the loan. Revenge-tinged rage rose up in Eliud, geyser-like, from an angry place like an uncapped well inside him. He grabbed the subcontractor around the neck, screaming, "Where's my money? Where is it?" Though the sub was a big, burly guy, he was no match for Eliud's rage. He threw the sub on the ground, screaming at him and choking him with those unsoiled, smooth hands of his until the sub's lips were lilac and his eyes bulged. Bile spent, Eliud summoned a cop and had his subcontractor arrested for robbery.

Then he went home and threw his family a party. He was off the hook for the building debt!

It didn't take but a few hours for the word of the scene in the street and the subcontractor's arrest to reach the king. The cops came right in the middle of the family party going on at Eliud's home and dragged the lot of them before the king.

Eliud had crumpled up the mercy he'd been given like it was a wad of filthy paper towels, tossing it aside with those unsoiled, smooth hands of his. He'd never really believed he needed it. His loan shark treatment of the subcontractor told the king that what this man really valued was justice. The king told Eliud angrily, "You want justice instead of mercy? It's yours, starting now."

Sitting in a prison cell that night, Eliud stared at his unsoiled, smooth hands. Those beautiful hands were about to become the rough, dirty hands of a slave ... after his will had been broken by the jailers who'd been given the job of torturing him into submission.

Before Jesus told this story, he'd been talking with his disciples about the best way to handle things when someone sinned against another person. He gave them a way to confront hurt that both addressed the hurt and offered protection to each party in a dispute (Mt 18:15–20). The thing he didn't give them was a promise that if they followed these steps, it was a guaranteed happy ending.

Jesus's friend Peter heard that omission loud and clear. So he asked Jesus the question, "Lord, how many times shall I forgive my brother when he sins against me? Up to seven times?"

Jesus's famous seventy times seven response isn't a math problem, it's an answer. He tells each of us that metering out "forgiveness" by the numbers isn't forgiveness at all. In God's upside down accounting system, Jesus tells us that we stop the free flow of mercy into our lives when we insist on trying to exact repayment from the one who has taken something from us unfairly. This flow of mercy is the true happy ending, not the temporary rush that comes with repayment extracted from another by revenge.

ParableLife: Payback

He took so much from her in just a few minutes time.

Cousin Jim stood at the doorway with 8-year-old Kelly and her two older brothers, waving goodbye as both sets of parents went out for dinner that early summer evening. Kelly's family was staying at Jim's family's home while they were in Iowa for the weekend visiting their hometown and church. Jim didn't have anything going on that evening, so he thoughtfully volunteered to watch Kelly and her brothers.

As well as being thoughtful, Jim was a model of trustworthiness—he was a twenty-something worship leader, a rising star in their denomination. He'd been groomed to take his place in the church since he was a little boy, continuing the family's multigeneration Christian heritage.

After the parents had left, Jim shooed Kelly's brothers outside to play before the sun went down. Kelly was sitting on the floor watching TV, and Jim sat on the couch behind her, after he'd locked the screen door. He told Kelly she was his favorite little cousin, so pretty and sweet, and she was going to be his special playmate tonight. If all the other cousins knew she was his favorite, he said, they'd feel left out. It would be OK this one time if this was their secret.

Then he pulled her onto his lap and stole her faith and her childhood from her.

The next morning, they went to church. They always went to church. It was the glue that held the sprawling extended family together. She sat between her smiling parents, watching them sing along with Jim, and she felt unprotected for the first time in her life. Parents are supposed to protect you, and last night they didn't.

She mechanically mouthed the words to the songs and watched Jim like she was watching a complete stranger. He'd glanced Kelly's way just once during the service that first morning after he'd sexually abused her, while he was singing a line about a holy God.

The abuse continued for five more years, happening each time Kelly's family went to Iowa to visit. It finally stopped when another cousin who lived in the same town as Jim came out with a story that tore the family apart. It seems that she'd been Jim's favorite, too, and he'd been abusing her regularly.

Then a few others at Jim's church came forward ... more

favorites. Jim confessed in the face of overwhelming evidence, and he ended up in prison.

Kelly saw how the extended family had flown apart like liquid in space when Jim went away, and she knew that she could never, ever tell anyone that Jim had done the same thing to her that he'd done to the others. After all, it had just been a few times. It was all in the past ... and maybe she'd asked for it somehow.

Right?

If only she could have stopped feeling so grimy inside.

Her parents stopped going to church. News traveled through the grapevine from Iowa to their Indiana town. In the wake of the pain and confusion that the family felt, it seemed easier to stay away for a while. The "for a while" became permanent just as Kelly hit her teen years.

In high school Kelly threw herself into sports and drinking with equal commitment. Sports gave her a feeling of complete command of her body. She liked that. On the other hand, when she wasn't on the playing field, she didn't want to feel anything. Drinking took care of that.

She didn't consciously spend any time thinking about the abuse. But sometimes she'd have dreams and she'd wake up and feel dirty and used. Nothing that couldn't be fixed by a drinking binge or sex. It was like trying to wash herself clean with mud.

By the time Kelly was a high school senior, she was tired of the soiled way she felt. She decided she needed a fresh start, so she chose a college in a nearby state where she didn't know anyone except Tom and Andrea, distant cousins who'd never really been a part of her life. It didn't take long for Kelly to discover that her old party girl habits were at home on the college campus. Her grades weren't great, but she managed to keep her GPA just over a 2.0 so she didn't lose her place on the college track team.

Tom and Andrea would occasionally invite her to their home for a decent, non-dorm meal. Tom and Andrea were old-school Christians, hewn straight from the trunk of the family tree. This meant they were kind, welcoming people who served every dinner with a side dish of Invitation To Come To Church With Us On Sunday Morning. She politely avoided these invitations, but they seemed unfazed by her excuses. She really did like them in spite of their squeaky-clean ways, so one frigid February Sunday of her sophomore year, she rolled out of bed three hours earlier than she normally did on a weekend (no hangover that morning, which helped) and went to church with them.

She hadn't been to church since she was a kid. She wept through the entire service that first day. Tom and Andrea occasionally offered her a gentle hug or a tissue. With amazing self-restraint, they didn't pry much about the cause of the tears.

Even if they had, Kelly didn't yet have the words to tell them. She hadn't really cried like that, ever.

A couple of weeks later, after a few weeks of solid partying and occasional class attendance, she agreed to go to church with them again. Tears again, slower this time, like a soaking rain. *Was this God?* Couldn't be. She'd dumped God from her life long ago. It was like she'd placed her idea of who God was in bagful of kitchen trash and hauled it out to the curb so that the garbage guys could haul him away.

After church this time, she decided that she wanted to tell Tom and Andrea about the darker side of her life at college. She felt weighed down somehow, and thought if she unburdened herself, she could wriggle free from the pressure inside of her. Maybe if she told them what kind of a person she really was ... maybe they'd been thinking she was a good Christian girl all this time. Maybe if they knew she wasn't ...

They listened without flinching. Their listening felt like love. She felt safe and, for a moment, nearly clean.

But by Sunday night in the dorm, when she washed down some Pop-Tarts with a couple of beers, the heavy, dirty feeling blanketed her again.

Throughout spring semester, she continued her same old ways but managed to attend church with Tom and Andrea many Sunday mornings. No matter how she tried to talk herself out of crying before she got there, the tears always worked themselves loose from her soul at some point during the service.

Her cousins began dragging her home after church, feeding her lunch (way better than dorm food), and talking about God and life with her. These meals were as much church for her as the worship, message, and communion of the service was.

The week after Easter, sitting around the kitchen table after lunch, Cousin Jim's name and crime came up in their conversation. This had happened a couple of times before, and Kelly had always refrained from commenting. But that Sunday afternoon, she spoke the words that had been bottled up inside of her for years, the words she'd never been able to say out loud before.

"He did it to me, too."

Tom and Andrea cried with her that afternoon. Their genuine sorrow over what had happened to her communicated more powerfully than all the compassionate words they spoke to her and prayed over her that afternoon. Their reaction reflected Jesus to her. Kelly had always suspected that he'd somehow been responsible for her pain, but she found herself thinking that maybe, just maybe, he wasn't. Maybe.

After that day, she started to read the Bible that Tom and Andrea had given her for her birthday earlier that year. She discovered someone very different from the image she'd had of God as either powerful abuser or impotent caretaker. She discovered that Jesus liked hanging around with people just like her. Instead of abandoning them or abusing them, he grabbed on to people and let them grab onto him, transforming hookers, sick people, crooks, thugs, and people trapped in the grip of Satan with powerful love. And he got in the faces of people who put on a front while they abused their power.

People like Cousin Jim.

Tom and Andrea kept speaking the truth to her about what had happened—Jim was sin-sick and perverted, none of it was her fault, and good could come out of this bad. "Why did this happen to me?" bubbled up in Kelly, free to surface after so many years of being submerged. Tom and Andrea had no glib answers but spoke of their trust in the power and character of God. But mostly, they listened.

Because of their prayerful listening, Kelly slowly became aware that God had given her the same choices he'd given to Jim. What had she done with her choices except choose to layer a lot of out-of-control behavior on top of Jim's abuse? She was responsible for the years of sex and drinking. Not Jim. Not God.

One Sunday night just before finals, she was driving from Tom and Andrea's to the library to study. Radio off, in the silence, she pulled over in the darkness and told God that she was tired of living the way she'd been living, feeling suffocated by the layers of grimy filth she understood now was sin. Cleansing tears spilled down her face as she asked God for the first time for the forgiveness Jesus offered from the cross.

There was a song they sang at Tom and Andrea's church that welled up from a place inside of her that she didn't know existed until she prayed that prayer:

> *I know a place, a wonderful place*
> *Where accused and condemned*
> *Find mercy and grace*
> *Where the wrongs we have done*
> *And the wrongs done to us*
> *Are nailed there with Him*
> *There on the cross ...*
>
> *At the cross, He died for my sin.*
> *At the cross, He gave me life again.*

—"At the Cross"
©1993 Mercy/Vineyard Publishing

"I don't want you going there, Kelly. What's it gonna change?" Kelly's mom chewed nervously on a loose cuticle. "Please, honey. Just forget about the whole thing."

Kelly couldn't blame her for feeling nervous. When Kelly had finally told her parents about Jim's abuse over Christmas break, they were devastated. Her dad had charged around like a bull in a red room, threatening to go over to Jim's house and beat him to a pulp. Her mom cried, fluttering moth-like around the house, treating Kelly as if she had announced she had a terminal illness.

Over the next days, Kelly had talked them both down from their respective emotional ledges, explaining over and over again that God had been healing the damage done to her and the damage she'd done to herself.

As if that bombshell wasn't enough, Kelly had gone and dropped this latest and biggest one when she came home for summer break a few months later: "I need to go and talk to Jim," she told them. "I want to tell him that I have forgiven him."

Kelly's mom's voice shook as she repeated the question, as if Kelly didn't hear it. "What's it gonna change?"

Kelly looked at her steadily, one determined tear tracing the side of her nose. (Would the tears ever stop?) "What's it gonna change? It's going to change *me*, mom."

He'd taken so much from her. She needed to tell him that he couldn't ever repay it, and he didn't have to.

She drove out to Iowa for the weekend, planning to stay with a friend from the campus fellowship group she had joined the past year. Her friend committed to pray for her while she went to see Jim. He was still living at home with his parents, working in a warehouse, and having regular meetings with his probation officer. He was shorter than she remembered, with a paunch and a receding hairline.

She didn't take her eyes from his face as she gave him the *Reader's Digest* version of what led to her commitment to live as a follower of Jesus. "He's forgiven me for so much," she said steadily. "I came here to tell you that I forgive you for what you did to me."

He couldn't meet her gaze. He mumbled, "I've done a lot of things I'm ashamed of in my life, Kelly."

She stood in silence for a moment, willing herself not to cry, remembering. Forgiving, and being forgiven. "I have, too, Jim. I have, too."

In Real Time

I've been hurt deeply in my life. But my wounds are in places different from Kelly's. There have been a few people along the way who wanted something from me and were willing to hurt me so that they could get it.

I bet you can say the same thing. Maybe your wounds have been financial. Or they've robbed you of a job. Perhaps the wounds have been in the form of relationships that turned on you and ruined your reputation. Worse yet, maybe people have cruelly mistreated you or abandoned you.

When we've been damaged by the actions of another, our first impulse is the desire to choke the life out of the person, screaming, "Give it back!" For some of us, this impulse becomes a permanent resident inside of our souls. It certainly did in the case of the servant of the king in the parable of the vigilante "victim" found in Matthew 18:21–35.

The costliest words, and the hardest to say and mean, are "I forgive you. You took _____ from me, and I'm releasing you from ever having to give it back to me. You can't pay me back, and you don't have to." It seems that the only way it is possible to say these words when the hurt is deep is to drop your hands from around the neck of the person you're choking, and reach toward your heavenly Father the way little children reach up to their parents to be held.

Innocent Jesus, who was (willingly) being put to death for a world of sin he didn't commit, reached for his Father with his soul from the cross. "When they came to the place called the Skull, there they crucified him, along with the criminals— one on his right, the other on his left. Jesus said, *"Father, forgive them, for they do not know what they are doing"* (Lk 23:33–34).

His death and resurrection offer each of us the power to drop our hands from the necks of those who have taken a piece of our lives from us and reach to God. Shortly after Jesus lived, one of his followers named Stephen was unjustly accused of preaching contempt for God and the Jewish law. It was a kangaroo court, and Stephen, figuring he was as good as dead anyway, took the opportunity to tell Jesus's story by reviewing highlights from the Old Testament that pointed toward him. At the end of his message, they stoned him. Stephen's response? "Stephen prayed, 'Lord Jesus, receive my spirit.' Then he fell on his knees and cried out, 'Lord, do not hold this sin against them.' When he had said this, he fell asleep" (Acts 7:59–60).

The resurrection makes it powerfully possible for us to forgive. God offers each of us forgiveness for the countless ways we have abused his goodness, trampling purity into the dirt by our wrong thoughts, words, and acts. Receiving this is the starting place and finishing line of each journey toward forgiveness.

The Message paraphrase of the Bible explains that the pattern of prayer Jesus gave his followers includes a cry for forgiveness: "In prayer there is a connection between what God does and what you do. You can't get forgiveness from God, for instance, without also forgiving others. If you refuse to do your part, you cut yourself off from God's part" (Mt 9:14–15).

The prayer that Jesus gave his disciples as a pattern for communication and communion with his Father offers each of us this same communication and communion with the Father as we pray it. You may find yourself powerless to your own urges to exact revenge against someone who has hurt you. When you invite God into that powerless place, you can receive the power to do this impossible thing. It is as simple and difficult as asking for help.

The following contemporary interpretation of the familiar prayer (often called "The Lord's Prayer") is from *The Message*. It strips each phrase of this petition to its essence. Take some time to journal the prayers that arise in you in response to each phrase of this prayer as you seek to forgive and reach for God:

> *Our Father in heaven,*
> *Reveal who you are.*
> *Set the world right;*
> *Do what's best—as above, so below.*
> *Keep us alive with three square meals.*
>
> *Keep us forgiven with you and forgiving others.*
> *Keep us safe from ourselves and the Devil.*
> *You're in charge! You can do anything you want!*
> *You're ablaze in beauty!*
> *Yes. Yes. Yes.*

—Matthew 6:9–13

Continue the Conversation:
How has unforgiveness affected the relationships in your life?

CHAPTER SIX

Dangerous Safety

How to Be a Lifeguard with Two Broken Arms

The Merciful Neighbor

On one occasion an expert in the law stood up to test Jesus. "Teacher," he asked, "what must I do to inherit eternal life?"

"What is written in the Law?" he replied. "How do you read it?"

He answered: "Love the Lord your God with all your heart and with all your soul and with all your strength and with all your mind"; and, "Love your neighbor as yourself."

"You have answered correctly," Jesus replied. "Do this and you will live."

But he wanted to justify himself, so he asked Jesus, "And who is my neighbor?"

In reply Jesus said: "A man was going down from Jerusalem to Jericho, when he fell into the hands of robbers. They stripped him of his clothes, beat him and went away, leaving him half dead. A priest happened to be going down the same road, and when he saw the man, he passed by on the other side. So too, a Levite, when he came to the place and saw him, passed by on the other side. But a Samaritan, as he traveled, came where the man was; and when he saw him, he took pity on him. He went to him and bandaged his wounds, pouring on oil and wine. Then he put the man on his own donkey, took him to an inn and took care of him. The next day he took out two silver coins and gave them to the innkeeper. 'Look after him,' he said, 'and when I return, I will reimburse you for any extra expense you may have.'

"Which of these three do you think was a neighbor to the man who fell into the hands of robbers?"

The expert in the law replied, "The one who had mercy on him."

Jesus told him, "Go and do likewise."

—*Luke 10:25–37*

Reloaded: Looking for Loopholes

Who are you scared of?

Gangbangers?

Foreigners?

Republicans?

Democrats?

For the Jews in Jesus's day, the Samaritans were on the short list of Scary Outsiders. The Samaritans were a weird half-breed mongrel mix of people who'd picked over the religion of the Jews like they were at a smorgasbord. More than 400 years before Christ, a bigwig Jewish priest decided he wanted a pagan wife. When he lost his day job because of this choice, he did what any self-respecting religious expert would do—he started his own religion.

His group of followers—the Samaritans—grew at the edges of the Jewish world like a tumor. There'd been some bloody religious battles between the two groups, and the Samaritans had even gone so far as to desecrate the holy place the Jews worshipped. The Samaritans were rabid in their devotion to their outsider status, and all the members of the surrounding communities, especially the Jews, knew the safest, holiest way to handle them was to stay miles away from them. After all, they were dangerous in just about every way. They knew that Samaritans wouldn't mind killing them on a bad day, and their screwy half-breed religious convictions would mess with the Jew's piety any day.

Any person with a half a brain in their head would know this.

So when Jesus was quizzed by a Jewish religious professional looking for a loophole in his teaching, he couldn't have picked a more shocking character to demonstrate the radical life to which he was calling them.

"Who am I really required to care for?" a religious man inquired of Jesus. "What is the least I can do and still be okay before God?"

The first thing Jesus did to answer this man's question was to take him out to dangerous terrain—this steep, inhospitable stretch of road to Jericho was a home to criminals. There were big risks involved in traveling this route. All of those listening to Jesus's answer understood that the ultimate cost for using the road had been exacted from a nameless, faceless traveler. The man in the story was robbed, beaten to a pulp, and left to die.

Jesus continues by telling about the two religious professionals who discover this bleeding, naked, mostly dead victim. Jesus's listeners knew that these men would only maintain their holy status if they stayed away from this man.

Touching a dead or dying man would render them "unclean." These were God's rules, after all, and rules were rules.

It's worth noting that God's rules also had provision built into them for those who failed to keep them. If these two religious pros wanted to stop, they could have. They could have chosen to address the spiritual consequences of touching this near-corpse before the God they claimed to love.

So when Jesus introduces a Samaritan to the story, an Outsider, to choose to do what the religious professionals wouldn't do, it stopped his hearers cold. The Samaritan gave his life away to this victim, not with chocolate-covered cherry sentiment, but in actions that cost him his own plans, time, and even his own religious position. The core of the Samaritan's religion was based on the same rulebook that the Jews were using.

Most of us think of the Samaritan as a Boy Scout type, doing his good deed for the day. Nothing could be further from the truth. When the Samaritan showed up at the inn, splattered with the victim's blood because he'd cleaned the stranger, bandaged him with strips of his own clothing, transported him to a place he could heal, and then paid the bill, this wasn't a merit badge.

This was the love of someone who knew what it meant to be a friend.

ParableLife: Team Samaritan

The beating came from a source I didn't expect. If I'd have seen it coming, I would have taken a different route and avoided the violence entirely.

"Hey, Michelle—Pastor Chuck asked me to see if you'd be interested in coming up with a script for this year's Good Friday service." Dave, his administrative assistant, pulled me aside after church. "He and I were talking, and we both agreed that it would be great to do something different this year."

The typical Good Friday service at the church usually meant the crucifixion, mimed to violin-soaked worship music. It meant that a skinny guy, who'd agreed to starve himself and not shave for a week before the service, would be nearly naked in front of the church, writhing on a giant wooden cross. It was time for something new.

"I'd love to try," I said. "Would you be okay with me writing something contemporary that would focus on the message of the cross in our lives?"

"Oh yeah, absolutely," he nodded. "Go for it."

I'd been learning the craft of scriptwriting, and the church had been a great, safe place to try some innovative ways of communicating Christ's story. On the front burner of this faith community, bubbling warmly and scenting the air with invitation, were a lot of creatives. The church attracted people who were hungry for truth and beauty, hungry to hear God's voice, present tense. The scent of real life drew my family and me there.

However, simmering on the back burner of the church was a rotting-from-the-inside-out leadership crisis. The decision-makers were paralyzed by power politics and a crisis of vision and direction for the church. Several years later, I was saddened but not surprised to learn that at least part of the paralysis back then was fueled by the secret life of a key member of the leadership team, a very dark and sinful secret life, that had held his heart hostage for years while he was supposed to be helping to guide the church.

I occasionally caught a whiff of that stench, but mostly I smelled the incense of others around me who'd chosen to let their lives be consumed with love for God.

A fully realized idea for a play emerged a couple of weeks later. That kind of thing doesn't happen very often, so when it does, I say "Thank you, Father, for the gift!" and start writing like a maniac. The play's message was that God was for the broken people of this world, and that a broken heart was mandatory equipment for Christ-followers.

Sounds pretty good so far, right? One of the main characters in the script was a pastor who'd gotten so enchanted with his own success that he figured he could live outside the boundaries of an honest, humble life. No one was beyond their own sin, I wrote. Not even the pastor in my script. But the message of the script was that no one—including the fallen pastor—was beyond the healing offered by Jesus's holy shredded body hammered to a cross.

After finishing a first draft, I decided that it would be a good idea to get some input from Dave and Pastor Chuck. If the script wasn't what they were hoping for, I'd just as soon scrap it and help with something else.

I called Dave first, and gave him the synopsis, read him some dialogue. He was full of cooing encouragement, with one postcard-sized caution flag: "Pastor Chuck might not like it. But come on over to our house Thursday evening. Chuck and Jill are coming over for dinner. Why don't you stop by later that evening and we can all take a look at it?"

I found out much later that Dave knew just what would happen.

The vibe in the room grew more and more sour as I read from the script to the group gathered around Dave's table. I hadn't quite finished when Pastor Chuck let me have it.

"Why would you write a thing like this? Are you saying I'm like this pastor? Are you accusing me of something?"

I calmly answered his questions, explaining how the script idea was generated (a gift!), what I felt the message was for audiences, and assuring him that I wasn't accusing anyone of anything. My answers just made him madder. Red in the face, he began yelling, questioning my motives, my husband's motives (important to note: My husband wasn't even there), and then, finally, attacking my character, my loyalty to the church and to Jesus.

Now would be a good time to ask why I didn't get up and leave as soon as he started to get abusive. I've asked myself the same thing. Best I can tell you, I really trusted Pastor Chuck. And there were three other people in the room, sitting silently, watching as his tirade continued for nearly a half an hour. I trusted them, too.

As soon as there was a break in the action, I took my leave, got in the car, and began to shake violently. I had been violated by his tirade and by the willingness of the others to watch it all happen in silence. I was wounded badly, beaten up by his angry, accusatory words and hemorrhaging trust.

When I got home, my husband kept saying, "I wish I'd gone with you … . I wish I'd gone with you … ."

I told him sadly I never imagined I would have needed a bodyguard.

In the weeks that followed, my husband and I sought out Dave and his wife to ask why they didn't do anything to stop Pastor Chuck's attack. His response: "Gee, I figured you knew that Pastor had a problem with his temper." (I didn't.) We also sat down with Pastor Chuck and his wife. His apology-less explanation for his behavior: "I was tired that night."

And their solution was to begin a campaign of gossip about me and my now-branded-bad attitude, in order to do damage control to their own reputations.

The real story here isn't about leadership abuse. I've met dozens of people who've suffered similar (and worse) experiences in abusive church situations. Some of those people have checked out of church. Others have checked out of Christianity altogether. Others stay, living with a kind of spiritual post-traumatic stress.

Some say they know non-Christians who are way kinder and less hypocritical than Christians. I've said this sometimes, too. The truth is that Christianity doesn't make people hypocritical, but unhealed wounds and an unbroken soul do. And there are some religious professionals who have learned to cover up those unhealed, unbroken places with a burka of knowledge, busyness or trusty clichés while they hustle off to Somewhere Better, hurrying past an injured one.

The real story here is that God sent a weird random team of Samaritans who stopped and rescued me when I was too shattered to move. They didn't show up all at one time, or follow a program that would get me back on my feet ("Seven Steps To Spiritual Renewal!"). But each of them, together, separately, cooperated with God's holy conspiracy to get me to a place of safety so that I could heal. Though Pastor Chuck and company used a lot of words over the years to tell me about Jesus, Team Samaritan showed me Jesus. Each one of them fleshed out a verb in Jesus's Samaritan story.[1]

Linda *stopped*. She squatted next to me in the dirt, completely unafraid of my mess. Linda had once been homeless and lived with her kids in a car for a while. God met her there, and she eventually found her way to our church. Though too many of us had treated her like a walking service project, she regularly shrugged off our project-based pities. She reminded me that

[1] Thanks to the anonymous contributor to the IVP Commentary who invited his readers to stop and notice each verb in his thoughtful study of this passage.

even though there were a few dangerous people at church, the friendships she had there made it the safest place she'd ever been in her life.

Friends hang out with each other. She squatted next to me when I laid there bleeding, praying for help, her big, rough hands open, like a beggar, waiting with me. Waiting for Jesus.

Mike was willing to *touch my wounds*. Years later, I figured I'd worked through the worst of it and was now all right. Really. But at an organizational meeting in a new church in a new state years later, I saw an image, up close and personal, that transported me in time to that terrible night at Dave's house.

I freaked out, running in circles and screaming inside, while simultaneously trying to maintain a calm, rational exterior. I reminded myself that now wasn't then, that these people weren't those other people, and forced myself to focus on the reason for the meeting.

I thought I was doing a pretty good job of keeping my little breakdown to myself, except for the fact that I'd begun shaking uncontrollably, just like I had that night in my car after Pastor Chuck's verbal beating. I hoped no one would notice.

Mike noticed. He gently asked me if everything was okay. I tried offering a brief explanation that would have allowed me to preserve my dignity, but I'm pretty sure that it sounded like the rantings of a crazy person. My chattering teeth didn't help the effect.

Mike stopped the meeting, asked the others there to gather around me, lay their hands on my shaking body, and pray. He'd been an elementary teacher for years, and he knew just what to do when someone got hurt at recess.

None of them knew what they were really praying about for me. But the Holy Spirit living inside of them knew, and he moved them to pray prayers of freedom and release that actually worked. They could have branded me an emotionally disturbed woman, and they'd have been right. Instead, fueled by compassion, they didn't brand me anything at all except one of them, a friend in need of prayer.

Ginnie *dressed my wounds*. She did it in a really inventive way. Using blueberry donuts instead of wine, she dabbed antiseptic on my open, festering lesions. Then she'd dump super-unleaded coffee over those wounds in order to dress them. She bandaged my wounds, protecting them far longer than I would have ever imagined it was necessary. She cares for them still.

Ginnie used to show up at my house with a box of these wickedly good donuts from a mom-and-pop donut joint in town. She knew I was a sucker for their blueberry glazed donuts, along with an espresso-strength cup of coffee.

She knew Pastor Chuck and company, and had formed some strong opinions about what had happened to me. Though she was sympathetic to my plight, she refused to allow me to ooze my sorry story as if it were a terminal condition.

She was pretty determined to get me to own my problems, addressing the growing bitterness that kept creeping into my life as things played themselves out at the church. She clearly saw the problems breeding there, but she also saw the flesh-eating bacteria settling into my wounds.

"Pastor Chuck and the rest of them, they were wrong," she'd tell me. "But you're wrong, too. You're getting bitter. And who wins then?"

Ouch.

She didn't just come over to eat donuts and hammer at me. She'd laugh with me, tell me stories, and ask me for advice. She refused to let me die of a secondary infection.

My husband and I had a couple of pairs of friends who *loaded me onto a mule and carried me to safety*. We all attended Pastor Chuck's church, but each of us found ourselves at a spiritual crossroads. One couple longed to be missionaries and couldn't quite figure out how to get there from here. The other couple was sorting through some complex family issues and needed direction for their lives. And my husband and I were trying to make sense of what had happened at Dave's house, the gossip that came in the wake of it, and how we could follow God through it all.

We decided to get together for dinner, to share our stories and seek God. And we did, weekly, for about a year and a half before each pair ended up relocating from that area. Given the fact that we were all struggling with alienation-themed problems, we could have easily degenerated into whining and gossip. Truth: It happened on occasion.

But we came together to pray, and pray we did. None of us had any great wisdom or counseling finesse. So we prayed, and the prayer of these friends rescued me like a lifeguard, carrying me away from the place of damaging impact to a place of safety, setting me before God.

Karen *ran an inn*. Her home was a safe place for a lot of people. She had no agendas for the dozens of visitors who crossed the threshold of her second-floor urban home other than offering friends and strangers good food, a decent glass of wine, and a place to rest. The root word for 'hospitality' is 'hospital,' and Karen's hospitality had a healing component to it.

Seventeenth century poet George Herbert wrote a series of sonnets about love. In this, his third one, he tells the story of the healing hospitality embedded in love:

> *Love bade me welcome, yet my soul drew back,*
> *Guilty of dust and sin.*
> *But quick-eye'd Love, observing me grow slack*
> *From my first entrance in,*
> *Drew nearer to me, sweetly questioning*
> *If I lack'd anything.*
>
> *"A guest," I answer'd, "worthy to be here";*
> *Love said, "You shall be he."*
> *"I, the unkind, the ungrateful? Ah my dear,*
> *I cannot look on thee."*
> *Love took my hand and smiling did reply,*
> *"Who made the eyes but I?"*
>
> *"Truth, Lord, but I have marr'd them; let my shame*
> *Go where it doth deserve."*
> *"And know you not," says Love, "who bore the blame?"*
> *"My dear, then I will serve."*
> *"You must sit down," says Love, "and taste my meat."*
> *So I did sit and eat.*

The sinner was welcome at Love's table, not as a groveling, unworthy servant, but as an invited guest. Karen had experienced this in her own life, and was committed to spending the rest of her life inviting people to come and sit at her table, where they could maybe taste Love for themselves. Her home was a hospital for me, and I regenerated physically and emotionally just because I hung out around her table. She called me her friend and made sure I knew I was welcome, even when I was a bloody mess.

There wasn't one drop of religious obligation in the way that Team Samaritan operated. There was only merciful, true friendship, offered because they loved God. And because they loved God, they could incarnate love by stopping, touching and dressing my wounds, loading me on a mule, and carrying me to the safety of an inn.

It was what the Samaritan would have done.

It was what Jesus would have done. In fact, it's exactly what he did.

In Real Time

How can you ever stay the same if you've risen from death to life because someone saved you?

If you've been rescued, you know just what it takes to rescue someone else. The story of the Samaritan's friendship would have been different if he had laid his hands on this dying stranger to pray and God had chosen to heal the dying man on the spot. God absolutely can and does work miracles.

However, Jesus told this story as an invitation to participate in a different kind of God-intervention. Our own past hurts are often where he shows up and asks us to become a member of Team Samaritan. Our rehabilitation becomes more complete as we watch the road ahead for others who are in pain and choose to express Jesus's love to them by stopping, by bathing their wounds, or by carrying them to a safe place so that they can heal.

Former Insider-Turned-Jesus-Following-Outsider Paul wrote, "I want to know Christ and the power of his resurrection and the fellowship of sharing in his sufferings, becoming like him in his death, and so, somehow, to attain to the resurrection from the dead" (Phil 3:10–11). We discover what it means to share in the sufferings of Christ through our own wounds and through a Samaritan-like willingness to share the suffering of others.

We learn Christ and experience the power of resurrection when we do.

Psalm 35 was written by David generations before Christ's life. David had been unjustly accused of things he didn't do by a king who knew he would eventually lose his power. As a result, David had to leave home and family and live as a fugitive. Through emotional beatings and physical persecution, David cried out for help from the only one who could save him.

If you've been hurt by a boss, by a spouse, by a child, by a friend, by a church, pray through Eugene Peterson's *The Message* paraphrase of Psalm 35 for yourself. The words are as real and immediate as a knife wound, and the cry for God's help is the genesis of healing in your life.

Next, pray through these words again, this time as a Samaritan. Intercede with God on behalf of someone you know who has experienced great pain. This is the best first step as you journey out on that dangerous road to Jericho.

Listen to the cry from the broken man lying in the middle of the road:

> *Harass these hecklers, God,*
> *punch these bullies in the nose.*

Grab a weapon, anything at hand; stand up for me!

Get ready to throw the spear, aim the javelin,
    at the people who are out to get me.
Reassure me; let me hear you say, "I'll save you."

When those thugs try to knife me in the back,
    make them look foolish.
Frustrate all those who are plotting my downfall.

Make them like cinders in a high wind,
    with God's angel working the bellows.

Make their road lightless and mud-slick,
    with God's angel on their tails.

Out of sheer cussedness they set a trap to catch me;
    for no good reason they dug a ditch to stop me.

Surprise them with your ambush—
    catch them in the very trap they set,
    the disaster they planned for me."

—Psalm 35:1–8

Listen to the kind of treasure that's been stolen:

When they were sick, I dressed in black;
    instead of eating, I prayed.

My prayers were like lead in my gut,
    like I'd lost my best friend, my brother.

I paced, distraught as a motherless child,
hunched and heavyhearted.

But when I was down they threw a party!
All the nameless riffraff of the town came
chanting insults about me.

Like barbarians desecrating a shrine,
they destroyed my reputation.

—Psalm 35:13–16

Listen to the belief that only God can save:

God, how long are you going to
stand there doing nothing?
Save me from their brutalities;
everything I've got is being thrown to the lions.

I will give you full credit when
everyone gathers for worship;
When the people turn out in force
I will say my Hallelujahs.

Don't let these liars, my enemies,
have a party at my expense,
Those who hate me for no reason,
winking and rolling their eyes.

No good is going to come from that crowd;
They spend all their time cooking up gossip
against those who mind their own business.

They open their mouths in ugly grins, mocking,
"Ha-ha, ha-ha, thought you'd get away with it?
We've caught you hands down!"

Don't you see what they're doing, God?
You're not going to let them get by with it, are you?
Not going to walk off without doing something, are you?

Please get up—wake up! Tend to my case.
My God, my Lord— my life is on the line.

Do what you think is right, God, my God,
but don't make me pay for their good time.

Don't let them say to themselves,
"Ha-ha, we got what we wanted."
Don't let them say,
"We've chewed him up and spit him out."

Let those who are being hilarious at my expense
Be made to look ridiculous.
Make them wear donkey's ears;
Pin them with the donkey's tail,
who made themselves so high and mighty!

—Psalm 35:17–26

Listen to what it means to be on Team Samaritan:

But those who want the best for me,
Let them have the last word—a glad shout!—and say,
over and over and over,

*"God is great—everything works together
for good for his servant."*

*I'll tell the world how great and good you are,
I'll shout Hallelujah all day, every day.*

—Psalm 35:27–28

Continue the Conversation:
Have you ever experienced a Team Samaritan rescue? Can you describe the experience and how it has affected you?

CHAPTER SEVEN

Sandy Granite

Why Choose an Inconvenient Life?

Two Builders

> Therefore everyone who hears these words of mine and puts them into practice is like a wise man who built his house on the rock. The rain came down, the streams rose, and the winds blew and beat against that house; yet it did not fall, because it had its foundation on the rock. But everyone who hears these words of mine and does not put them into practice is like a foolish man who built his house on sand. The rain came down, the streams rose, and the winds blew and beat against that house, and it fell with a great crash.
>
> —*MATTHEW 7:24–27*

> Why do you call me, "Lord, Lord," and do not do what I say? I will show you what he is like who comes to me and

hears my words and puts them into practice. He is like a man building a house, who dug down deep and laid the foundation on rock. When a flood came, the torrent struck that house but could not shake it, because it was well built. But the one who hears my words and does not put them into practice is like a man who built a house on the ground without a foundation. The moment the torrent struck that house, it collapsed and its destruction was complete.

—*Luke 6:46–49*

Reloaded: Stoics on Steroids

As he walked through the nightmarish pile of debris that just hours ago had been his dream home, his face had the stunned expression that accompanies the shock of loss. His family had gotten out safely, just as the front edge of the storm tore into the house. They'd run for their lives away from the lashing wind, taking shelter in a small cave on the leeward side of the rocks lining the beach.

And now they had nothing left but the clothes on their backs.

Once the storm had passed, he sent his family into the nearby town to stay with relatives, far away from the risk and beauty of the wild shore. He walked slowly along the beach, eyeing what was once his carefully constructed dream. Pieces of the dream now littered the sandy shore. Beautiful hefty cedar beams, imported stone and tile, hand-wrought ironwork. Nothing but the best.

Now nothing at all.

He'd built his palace on this beautiful slice of shoreline. His children had played in the sand right outside their front door. The same sand served as a foundation for his house.

A couple of business associates had mentioned that sane people didn't build in such a dangerously beautiful location: Didn't he know that terrifying storms came from nowhere and slammed into that coastline?

He laughed at them and told them it had been years since a storm had hit his homesite. Besides that, he wasn't just anyone. He worked hard and lived right. He deserved this house. His monument to his own resourcefulness was its own insurance that no storm could ever affect his life plan.

It was the kind of insurance, he discovered, that left one bankrupt and homeless.

There are two similar but different accounts of the story of the two builders in the Bible. In both cases, Jesus tells the story as a punctuation mark at the end of his teaching about what it means to truly follow God. His teaching in Matthew 5–7, commonly known as the Sermon on the Mount, is a paradigm-shifting exposition that says that the Biblical law most of his hearers had always known (maybe not followed, but knew) was a harder, deeper reality than they'd ever imagined. He offers truth after truth to prove his point, telling his hearers things such as "Adultery isn't something you do—it begins in you the moment lust sparks the flint of your heart"; "Showing off your 'righteousness' for an audience is a fool's game—it doesn't net you a thing with God".

Luke 6:17–49 captures a shorter message that some Bible scholars call the Sermon on the Plain. Jesus had stopped alongside a level piece of highway to teach the crowds that followed him in hopes of catching a miracle in action. His message there is a similar, though condensed, version of the Sermon on the Mount.

The religious professionals had always taught that in order to build a life pleasing to God, the people needed to control their behavior in the way prescribed. Jesus knew it was easier to prescribe behavior controls than to talk about the condition of our rebel hearts. His sermon words were aimed directly at our rebel hearts.

Jesus knew that some who heard him talk about the behavior of someone who'd been changed from the inside out would attempt to turn the improved behavior into newer, harder rules. Be excellent to one another! *Or else*!

Those words weren't intended to build a new religious class of people who were little more than Stoics on steroids, syrupy-sweet Stepford Wives who are nice to restaurant waitstaff and rude drivers. Jesus was not preaching principles for better living. He was telling us that the only way to live the kind of live to which he is calling us is by digging deeply into him in a life-giving relationship.

The storm will come. Both Luke's and Matthew's stories tell us as much. It is a certainty. There are storms of confusion, persecution, loss, and pain that get unleashed in our individual lives. And there will be ferocious storms that will sweep across the earth as we approach the end of things, shaking loose everything that isn't anchored properly.

Skipping the hardest step of the construction process—digging into rock to create a foundation—might seem like it would save a lot of time and sweaty effort. But in the end, only the structure anchored to rock will stand. Sturdy building materials alone will not create a structure that can withstand a raging storm.

Jesus promises that he is the one foundation that can hold any structure built, no matter what storms may come. And his promise is rock-solid.

ParableLife: The Scoreboard

Wrigley Field, home to the Chicago Cubs, is the ultimate old-school ballpark. Built in 1914 and tucked into a trendy urban neighborhood on the city's north side, some are convinced that the ballpark has as many fans as the team itself. Today's ballparks are built along expressways and surrounded by acres of parking lots. Wrigley is a part of its neighborhood's fabric. It would be impossible to replicate Wrigley's ambience and location today.

Watching a game at Wrigley Field is a time warp experience. There weren't any night games played there until 1988, and it is still the kind of place that reminds you of newsreel sports footage from the 1940s, when men in fedoras sat in the hot sunshine watching the Cubbies get clobbered.

The scoreboard at Wrigley is another relic of a bygone era. The present scoreboard was erected in 1937, and it is still manually operated. There are people who sit inside the scoreboard, watching the game from the best seat in the house, and changing the numbers every time something new happens on the field.

Play by play, inning by inning, eventually each spot on the board is filled in by hand until the game is over. Cardinals 3, Cubs 1. The guys inside the board spell out a message in the sky each game day, and everyone who looks at it never questions that the information on the board is truth.

Steve pulled on his uniform and looked in the mirror. He totally looked like a Big League baseball player. He could almost hear the ballpark announcer introducing him: "And at shortstop, batting in the clean-up position for the Cubs is number 18, the mighty Steve Harris." The crowd went wild! He ran around his room, fists pumping.

"Stevie," his dad called up the stairs. "You better get a move on or you'll be late." His dad's voice snapped 10-year old Steve back to reality. Grabbing his cap and brand-new baseball shoes, he thundered down the stairs and jumped into the car with his dad.

They drove over to the Little League field, and Steve's dad pulled the car into the parking lot. "Have fun," his dad said. "I'm going to go run some errands. See you after the game."

He wasn't staying to watch the game? Steve got out of the car and stood stiffly in the parking lot as his dad drove away. His teammates were trickling onto the field while their families wandered into the bleachers to find their seats.

Steve swallowed the baseball-sized lump in his throat. It thudded into the pit of his stomach, where it stirred up the nervous butterflies that were already hard at work before this, his very first game. He told himself it didn't matter if his dad stayed or not, then ran to join his teammates for warmups before the game.

Just before he fell asleep that night, visions of the day's winning game flashing across his memory. He imagined the scoreboard at Wrigley Field, the one he'd seen on TV hundreds of times. In the windows that awaited each inning's score for the Cubbies, it looked like someone had swapped out some of the numbers and replaced them with letters. It looked like a message of some kind:

I—D O—

Steve didn't understand what it meant. Just as quickly, it vanished from his mind's eye as he tumbled into a dream.

As the season rolled on, he observed sadly that he was the only kid on his team who never had a family member come to watch a game. The other kids never seemed to notice, so he pretended not to notice either.

His mom and dad weren't there when he made an amazing double-play that saved the game. They weren't there when he struck out at the top of the ninth. They weren't there when he got hit with a line drive and ended up with a bloody nose. They never explained why their errands or their yard work couldn't wait, and he never asked.

Just before he fell asleep at night, that Wrigley Field scoreboard would flash through his mind. More letters filled the blank windows, halfway to completing the message:

I—DO—NOT—

I do not what? I do not eat broccoli? I do not like Language Arts?

The message was very mysterious, but left him feeling sad and alone, and he didn't know why.

Steve's team went to the playoffs at the end of the season, finishing in a very respectable third place. Coach Thompson pulled him to one side after the final game was over and the congratulations had faded away. "Steve, I just want you to know that you've been a key player on this team all season long," he began. "You put in great effort, buddy. One hundred and ten percent." There was a crunch of gravel in the parking lot bordering the field. Steve glanced toward the sound and saw his dad's car pull in. Coach Thompson watched Steve carefully, and he measured his next question cautiously before asking. "How many from your family are planning to come to the team pizza party next weekend? We have a lot to celebrate, and I'm looking forward to telling your folks what a fine player you've become."

He could see Steve swallow hard before steeling himself to answer. "No one from my family will be there, Coach."

What kind of a family did this kid come from? The parents always managed to get him to and from the games, but never once did either of them stay to watch him play. Heartbreaking. Coach Thompson said gently, "Gee, son, I'm sorry to hear that. I'd like to tell them both what a great job you did this season. I guess I'll just have to tell your dad right now. Let me walk you over to your car."

He trailed behind Coach Thompson on the long walk to his waiting dad. As he approached his dad's car, an image flashed across his soul, right there in broad daylight. It was a message from his dad on the Wrigley Field scoreboard, every blank filled in:

I—DO—NOT—CARE

Steve didn't play baseball the next season, or ever again. He attempted a variety of other activities over the next few years: Trombone lessons, Tae Kwon Do, Boy Scouts. Each of those activities seemed to be a promise that maybe something he did would matter to someone. To them.

His parents willingly paid for whatever he wanted to try, but they never showed a single drop of interest in anything he did. These polite, disinterested strangers seemed too busy with their own lives and issues. He heard the message loud and clear; he was an afterthought to them. The four-word message was always the same: I—DO—NOT—CARE.

Eventually, he stopped trying to do anything new, choosing the path of least resistance as he plodded through junior high and high school. There was enough duty in the discipline of his upbringing that he always managed to stay out of trouble. He ended up in the emergency room twice toward the end of high school suffering from panic attacks, but the doctors and his parents chalked it up to test anxiety.

Steve's curiosity was piqued the summer after his senior year when a couple of his coworkers at his landscaping job started talking about Jesus like he was some kind of a real person. Steve went out and got himself a Bible. He read it the way he read mystery novels: first skimming through the first third of it to figure out what the plot was, then reading the ending to find out if everyone lived happily ever after or what. A lot of the Bible seemed pretty intense, but reading it made Steve wonder what Jesus had to do with the beginning and the end. He then read through the Gospel of Matthew in three days, and discovered that Jesus had everything to do with all of it.

When he finished the last words of Matthew, where Jesus said, " ... surely I am with you always, to the very end of the age" (Mt 28:20), Steve told God that he wanted to follow him, too, just the way his coworkers did.

Those coworkers were thrilled about his decision and invited him to come with them to church. He began attending faithfully, quietly melting into the background just like he'd done all through school. He learned the songs, read the Bible, and prayed the prayers.

Steve grappled with some of the things the people said at church. He could understand all the stuff they said about people being sinners: He'd spent his whole life feeling like he could never quite get things right, so, somehow, the sin talk made sense to him. What didn't make sense to him at all was the way they were always talking about how the Father loved each one of them. Loved *him*.

He'd had a lifetime of practice not asking questions of people who were supposed to love him and couldn't, and sure didn't want to alienate the nice people at church with his doubts and fears. Steve swallowed hard and forced this latest bubble of anxiety down inside of him. He kept doing what he needed to do to be a good Christian.

A couple of years later, he married a cheerful, outgoing girl named Shellie whom he met at church. They settled into a careful, comfortable life peppered with work, church activities, and Shellie's Thursday night bowling league.

Sometimes, he dreamed about that Wrigley Field scoreboard. The "I do not care" message sent to him over and over and over by his parents had shriveled his self-confidence, though he never consciously thought about it during his waking hours. Steve was sure he'd never get a promotion at work, even though everyone there said he was more than qualified. It was safer to just not try for it. He struggled to trust that his wife loved him, even though she told him so daily. And though they attended a small group from church, he never said much, certain that no one really cared what he might have to add to the discussion.

Then he lost his job. The whole division had been outsourced. He'd worked there since the summer after high school. It was the one thing that had given his days a sense of stability.

To him, unemployment felt like God was telling him, "I do not care." The Wrigley Field scoreboard message spilled from his troubled dreams into his waking hours as his joblessness dragged on for weeks, then months. He didn't know how to tell anyone about the anxiety that rose up inside of him during those long empty days, not even Shellie.

Steve got sick of being in the spotlight at small group each week. "How's it going?" they'd ask. He'd answer politely, telling them that nothing much was happening, and then shrink back into the background as quickly as possible to beat the panic back down inside of him.

Gently, their friends from the group cared for the couple in small, practical ways. Groceries on the front step. Invitations for dinner or to watch movies. Anonymous checks in the mail. And though no one from the group had ever planned it, it turned out that each of them had begun praying every day for a breakthrough for Steve.

One warm May day, Steve helped Jeff roof his garage. A friend from small group, Jeff noticed that Steve had even smiled and laughed a few times as they worked together. It had been too long since he'd heard that laugh.

When they broke for lunch that day, the two of them leaned against the house, soaking in the sun for a few minutes. Jeff broke the long, companionable silence with a question: "Hey Steve—would you mind if I prayed for you?"

Steve just felt like he was shoved onto center stage, when just a moment earlier it had been two friends enjoying a near-perfect day. Why did Jeff have to drag God into it right this moment? Steve glanced at him and relaxed a little bit before answering. Jeff had been his friend for years, since that first summer after high school. He wasn't trying to shove Steve anywhere—he was just being Jeff, trying to care. "Sure, man," he nodded. "Uh ... thanks."

Jeff began to pray, thanking God for his friendship with Steve. Then, suddenly, before he even got to what was first and foremost on Steve's mind—a job—his flow of words came to a screeching halt in mid-sentence. Steve looked up from his hunched posture, and Jeff said, "I don't know exactly why I'm saying this, but I feel like you gotta hear that God loves you. He loves you. He's not your parents. He was there, even when they weren't."

A shock of recognition shot through Steve. No one knew about his parents' emotional abandonment of him, not even Shellie, and certainly not Jeff. Steve's parents now lived in another state, and he rarely talked about his childhood with her or anyone else. How could Jeff know?

"I hope I'm not off base, dude," Jeff said. "I don't even know your parents."

Steve could barely talk. "No," he whispered hoarsely. "You're not off base."

Jeff put his hand on Steve's shoulder and continued to pray for him. But Steve didn't hear a word that Jeff prayed after that. Jeff's heaven-aimed words mixed with the rush of wind that was shaking loose some of the letters from that Wrigley Field scoreboard in his soul.

God was sending him a different message from the one that had been there all this time.

Steve ... I—do—care.

In Real Time

Many of us have built at least part of our lives on a foundation of lies.

For example, even if we had the greatest parents in the world, they weren't able to parent us perfectly. They made choices based on their own mix of good experiences and broken places. Their decisions are perceived by each of us differently, based on our own personality, life experience, and the broken places that reside deep inside each one of us. A midnight curfew might hit one teen in a family as fair-minded grace ("They trust me!"), and her wild child sibling as a suffocating, cruel rule ("They don't trust me!"). The parents might have been trying to communicate confidence in their teen's growing maturity, but the wild child hears only suspicion.

Based on that perception, a whole pre-fab house of alienation can get erected on a foundation of suspicion in no time. Sadder is when the suspicion was never there to begin with. Its existence is a lie that becomes the basement of a life that's built in the wrong place.

We've all got them, those lies that form a sandy foundation for our own choices. It takes a lot of courage to ask God to show you where the lies might be laying under the choices you make in your life.

He will show you, sometimes in an epiphany and other times through the ferocity of storms. God allows the tumult to come, in love, so that he can shake loose everything built in the wrong place.

The puzzle of those storms is that some of them can irrevocably change the landscape of our lives as the fury of death, loss, and disease rip into our lives. There are no quick, glib answers for the "Why?" that is left standing when our lives are a wreckage.

The book of Job, nearly smack dab in the middle of the Bible, invites each one of us to ask painful, hard questions about the storms that tear our lives apart. You may find that the language of a contemporary translation, such as the *New Living Translation*, or a paraphrase, such as *The Message*, helps you hear the heart of God's message in Job in an accessible way.

After listening to Job and his friends try like forensics experts to dissect the tragedy that's befallen Job, God speaks. Twice, as God responds to their theories and questions, it is worth noting that he answers Job from a storm (Job 38:1, Job 40:6). God's answers aren't tidy little ovals that can be blackened with a number two pencil. There is not an easy way to explain the testing and trial in our lives.

Starting in Chapter 38 of Job and continuing to the end of the book, God responds to Job's anguished questions by not answering them directly. Instead, God responds with some questions of his own that challenge Job simply to look at him and what he's created.

Even though the book seems to have a mostly happy ending (Job passes the test and gets a lot of lovely parting gifts), the point of Job's story doesn't seem to be as much about the happy ending as it is about Job's discovery of who God is. Job's losses devastated him, but the revelation of who God is humbled him: "My ears had heard of you but now my eyes have seen you. Therefore I despise myself and repent in dust and ashes" (Jb 42:5, 6).

One look at God changed everything for Job. Though Job didn't receive direct answers to the questions he'd asked God, he received truth that changed the way he perceived everything about his life and his Maker. That truth is a granite foundation that will withstand every storm.

Continue the Conversation:
In what ways is your experience of God at odds with what the Bible says about his character?

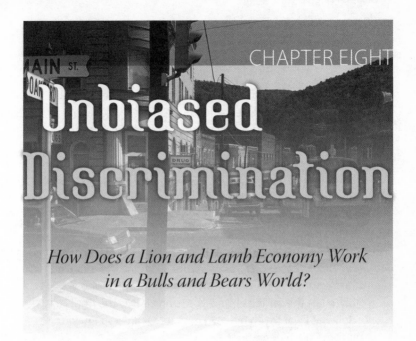

CHAPTER EIGHT

Unbiased Discrimination

How Does a Lion and Lamb Economy Work in a Bulls and Bears World?

A Day's Work for a Day's Pay ... Or Not

For the kingdom of heaven is like a landowner who went out early in the morning to hire men to work in his vineyard. He agreed to pay them a denarius for the day and sent them into his vineyard.

About the third hour he went out and saw others standing in the marketplace doing nothing. He told them, "You also go and work in my vineyard, and I will pay you whatever is right." So they went.

He went out again about the sixth hour and the ninth hour and did the same thing. About the eleventh hour he went out and found still others standing around. He asked them, "Why have you been standing here all day long doing nothing?"'

"Because no one has hired us," they answered.

He said to them, "You also go and work in my vineyard."

When evening came, the owner of the vineyard said to his foreman, "Call the workers and pay them their wages, beginning with the last ones hired and going on to the first."

The workers who were hired about the eleventh hour came and each received a denarius. So when those came who were hired first, they expected to receive more. But each one of them also received a denarius. When they received it, they began to grumble against the landowner. "These men who were hired last worked only one hour," they said, "and you have made them equal to us who have borne the burden of the work and the heat of the day."

But he answered one of them, "Friend, I am not being unfair to you. Didn't you agree to work for a denarius? Take your pay and go. I want to give the man who was hired last the same as I gave you. Don't I have the right to do what I want with my own money? Or are you envious because I am generous?"

So the last will be first, and the first will be last.

—*MATTHEW 20:1–16*

Reloaded: Money for Nothing

It was going to be a warm one. Even before the sun cracked the horizon, he could feel the heat radiating from the warm, rich soil. Today's sun was the ingredient that would coax his grapes into perfect readiness.

Last night, as he'd walked through his sprawling vineyards sampling grapes to assess their condition, he knew that today was going to be the day. Winemaking was as much art as it was science. And though the scientist in him said he might be able to wait another day or two, the artist in him said that this would be the day his grapes would be ready. It was his artistry with fruit and sunshine and cask that gave him a reputation throughout the region as a master vintner.

He needed some day laborers, so he headed to the marketplace where strong men with strong backs congregated looking for work. He needed men who wouldn't need to be nannied, but who'd work hard without complaining until the day was done.

His experienced eye was as good at judging workers as it was at judging grapes. He gathered a willing group, offering them the going rate for the day's work.

As the blazing sun rose higher in the sky, he intuitively sensed that the sugars in his grapes were coming to the peak of flavor. Another day or two on the vines, and he knew that his wine would take on a slightly moldy, overripe taste. He could still sell the wine when it was ready, but he didn't make his reputation as a manufacturer of fine wine by selling second-rate product.

Time was of the essence, so mid-morning he returned to the marketplace to recruit some more workers. When he saw so many willing men still looking for work at that hour, he thanked the Creator of the fruit of the vine, the fruit that these men would soon be harvesting. He offered this group of workers the same pay he'd offered to the men who'd been working for him since sunrise. The smiles on their faces in response to his offer were a promise that they'd work just as hard as the others, even though this group was the B team.

Just before noon, he stood on the patio behind the main house on his property. Though there wasn't a cloud in the sky, he felt the wind shift almost imperceptibly. He sensed that the weather was going to change. Rain was coming. A hard rain could change this perfect harvest into a total loss. A sense of urgency rose in him.

He hiked back to the marketplace. There were still a small number of men sitting in the shade, trying to stay cool. Though no one came looking for workers at high noon, the men there had chosen to wait there, hoping to connect with potential employers who might be seeking their next workday's help.

The looks on these men's faces were priceless when he asked them if they'd be willing to work half the day for a full day's pay. Of course, they said. Absolutely! Though they weren't a dream team, his offer transformed them into willing workers.

A few thin clouds skittered across the sky as the day blazed on. Midafternoon, he went back to the marketplace to hire a few more men. The men still hanging around there were older, or were in third-rate physical condition.

When he told them that he'd pay them the going rate for an entire day's work, they glanced at one another as if they'd heard something outrageous, which they had. As he led them from the marketplace toward his vineyards, he glanced over his shoulder at the handful of mostly broken old men still hoping for work. He nodded to himself and smiled.

He came back just before quitting time and told the lot of them that if they came with him, he'd pay them just like they'd worked for him the entire day. They wouldn't have time to do much more than pull a few clusters of sweet, warm grapes off of the vine. It was no more work than they would have done to feed themselves.

As the sun sank into the shadowed hills, the wind shifted again and a flash of heat lightning streaked across the plum sky. His gut had been right. Today was the day the harvest needed to happen, and it had, thanks to a small army of day laborers. He breathed a prayer of thanksgiving to his Lord, the Lord of the harvest.

He asked them to fall into line so he could pay them, organizing themselves in the sequence in which they were hired. He handed each one of them the exact same amount of money.

The first group in line, the men who'd worked one hour, fell over themselves thanking him for his kindness.

His midafternoon hires were nearly as effusive in their gratitude. The noon guys were quietly grateful, but a few of them passed quizzical looks between themselves.

The midmorning guys were mostly silent as they held their hands out to receive what they had coming to them.

The sunburned men who'd been working for him since the crack of dawn couldn't hold back their disdain. "How could you pay the guys who only worked one hour the same amount of money you paid us? They haven't done squat compared to us!" They'd worked so hard, and some of these afternoon hires hadn't done much of anything.

Anything, that is, except follow him.

Jesus's disciples had poured their lives into following him. They'd been with him since the dawn of his ministry.

They listened in horror as Jesus told the bald truth to a man who was trying to figure out how he could follow him while schlepping a financial security blanket behind him like an adult Linus from the Charlie Brown comic strip. Jesus told the man it was impossible to follow him like that.

That's when Jesus's friend Peter piped up. "Jesus, we've given up everything for you. There is no security blanket for us. So ... isn't there gonna be some kind of reward for us?"

Jesus told Peter that yes, there would be amazing eternal rewards that he couldn't possibly imagine. He understood that they'd left behind their own security blankets to follow him, but that didn't entitle them to a prize. There was no point system operating here.

Jesus's friends had a foretaste of their eternal reward as their lives were changed by following him, in the sweet here and now of being with him and learning his ways. There would be a reward just as sweet for those who came to him with their dying breaths. This was his new economy, an economy based entirely on grace. Jesus offered provision for everyone who was willing to follow Him, whether it was for their whole lives or their final breaths.

He began his parable with words that shatter the idea that our performance or achievement gives us an edge with God: "But many who are first will be last, and many who are last will be first" (Mt 19:30).

After telling the story of the generous boss, Jesus made sure that his audience heard him loud and clear, by ending the story the same way he started it, with the words: "So the last will be first, and the first will be last" (Mt 20:16).

ParableLife: Classified Ads

The loneliest five minutes of my week last summer were the five minutes after the church service ended. That final "Amen" meant that most of the congregation exploded out of their seats like each one was being fired from a missile silo. Most of these human missiles had homing devices that zeroed in on their peers. Young parents spoke together in busy, casual shorthand as they made their way to pick up the little ones from their Sunday morning activities. Teens clustered in a corner, acting out the high drama of youth group relationships. Older couples clustered in groups of four or six, chatting about their kids, an upcoming mission trip to Mexico, lunch at a nearby restaurant.

After that "Amen," my husband Bill and I would pull on our coats slowly, scanning the room for a face that was looking for us. No one was. We'd fidget with our cell phones or take another moment to reread the bulletin one more time, hoping for a human connection. We were glad to be there to worship God, but I tell you, it felt uncomfortable being there when no one else seemed to care if we showed up.

Especially during those five minutes after the service ended.

I think it might be helpful to mention the fact that crowds don't scare me. I'm a big time extrovert. My mom used to say that if you stuck me in a room with fifty strangers, an hour later I'd emerge knowing something about all fifty. My husband is more of an introvert by nature, but he's picked up an extrovert habit or two from hanging around me all this time. So neither one of us is a wallflower.

After the service ended, we'd try initiating conversations or asking questions. Once in a while, someone would make a little small talk with us on their way out the door: "Boy, that sunshine sure is bright today." But most weeks, we came and went as if we were invisible.

Years earlier, when we had relocated to Wisconsin, we'd gone through the same thing. We really were strangers in a strange land, searching for a healthy, welcoming church. We longed to be a part of a congregation where we could learn about God from servant-leaders we could respect, worship him together with others, make some friends and find meaningful ways to serve our new neighbors.

We found a church that seemed to fit the bill. When we first began attending, we tried to figure out how to move beyond this hour or so on Sunday morning to learn how to become part of the faith community. Our first road map into the landscape of the congregation was the church bulletin.

Lots of churches hand people a bulletin when they walk in the door on Sunday mornings. The bulletin might be a Xeroxed sheet full of spelling errors or a typeset masterpiece, but the content really isn't all that different from place to place. It's a news brief of the life of the church that week, and includes stuff like a list of babies born, notes about who has died, information about the theme of the service that day. And there are announcements, invitations to participate in the life of the church:

> College and Career Group—Sunday 7 p.m.
> Mandatory Children's Ministry meeting—
>   Thursday 7 p.m.
> Nursery workers needed for both services—
>   Call the church office for more info.
> Intercessory Prayer before the service—
>   8:30 a.m. each Sunday in Room 207
> Small group leadership training—
>   Saturday morning 9–12.
> Women's retreat deposits due in the church
>   office no later than this Wednesday.

I felt like I was looking at specially coded classified ads when I read most church bulletins. Maybe I needed a pair of those green and red 3-D glasses to see the real picture. If I squinted my eyes just right, I could distinctly see ads that read like these:

> Help Wanted: Support our organization and develop important servant skills at the same time. We need YOU! Thankless tasks include: Babysitters for the church nursery during Thursday morning women's bible study, cleaners for the church bathrooms, cutting the church lawn and more. Call 555-5555 immediately!

Needed: Motivated individuals willing to commit to organization-sponsored training workshops. (Okay, we mean commit to attending one of our Bible studies.) No experience required. Teachable spirit and regular attendance a necessity. Curriculum available for all age groups and skill levels. Enhance your life with learning! Call 555-5555 today!

White-collar opportunity available: If you're a team player—a highly motivated self-starter with organizational experience, creativity and well developed problem solving skills—we have a management position waiting for you with our growing organization. You've shown us what you have by serving and learning, working your way up the ladder around here— now put your knowledge, gifts, and talents to work with us as a leader! Don't call us, we'll call you.

Bill and I wanted to experience community, serve God, and experience spiritual growth. The church told us that all of this would happen as we began answering the first two types of ads. We worked in the nursery. We served as greeters. We hosted small groups in our home. We attended conferences and seminars. We got involved in prayer ministry.

Much later, I realized that though we were answering "Help Wanted" ads that often filled slots on the church organizational chart, I'd read between the lines and wishfully imagined that we were also answering personal ads in the process. No, not one of those "Men Seeking Women" ads—

but G-rated, platonic ads that simply read "Friend Seeking Friend."

We got real busy. Our phone rang constantly, and our calendar was full. We had purpose, we had relationships.

Or did we?

Besides those organizational charts that sometimes seemed to fly in the face of the organic structure the Bible describes in Paul's first letter to his friends at Corinth (1 Cor 12–13), there is another organizing principle at work in many churches. People seem to relate to one another like a little solar system. The pastor, staff, and key church leaders are at the core, playing the role of the sun, exerting a gravitational pull on the rest of the congregation.

Out at ring one, circling closest to the sun, are the congregation's movers and shakers, the ones who have easy access to those at the core. Ring one people know how to make things happen in the church.

In the next ring, circling farther out from the sun but still steadily orbiting it, are the good soldiers who shovel the church parking lot, support programs, bring casseroles to new moms, serve as ushers, and cheerfully attend Bible study each week.

Still farther away from the core is the third ring, those who attend Sunday services pretty regularly, but otherwise hold back from much commitment.

Then there are a few people who circle crazily like a meteor belt around the edge of this solar system. These are the people who called the church home but hadn't successfully answered an ad to move themselves into any kind of regular orbit. The "sun's" take on these folks was that they'd be a whole lot more stable and healthier spiritually if they'd just read the bulletin and get with the program.

We got to know some of these people, and it seemed like some of them would never be able to get with the program as it was advertised:

Sharon had spent most of the last fifteen years of her life bouncing in and out of mental health centers. She'd had a series of breakdowns in her mid-twenties as a young mom and had been kissed with the diagnosis that she was schizophrenic, along with a constellation of other secondary diagnoses. She spent the middle part of her life journeying through a forest of voices that tormented her, and a forest of medical professionals who tried to make the voices stop. She met Christ while watching a televangelist and it took every drop of her strength to simply hold on to Jesus with her shaking hands, a result of the banquet of shock treatments and chemicals that had promised (and failed) to fix her.

Frank was wheelchair bound and lived in a nursing home. Before his MS turned into an aggressive Pac-Man that ate the ends of his nerve coverings for lunch, Frank had been a husband, a father, an employee. His wife had left him as his physical condition deteriorated. Though his mind was still sharp, it was trapped inside a deteriorating body that wouldn't listen to the signals his brain tried sending to his muscles.

John was glad to orbit all the crazy church activity from a nice safe distance. He was convinced that most of it was busywork invented to keep people on an activity treadmill. He refused to be manipulated into doing a bunch of busywork to prove he was spiritual.

Others tried to answer the church want ads, but they disqualified themselves. These folks really did want to get with the program, but the program couldn't accommodate the round-peg people who wanted to serve but didn't fit the square holes the church had to offer:

Jerry was a loud, opinionated man who hadn't had a drink in four years, three months, twelve days, seventeen hours, and three minutes. He'd come a long way in that time, but years of alcoholism had taken its toll on his personality. Now that he was no longer anesthetized, he was experiencing emotions he'd never felt before. This meant that he often had the finesse of a rhino at a tea party.

When he first came to the church, he was a good project for those at the core and in rings one and two. But after all his time there, the glacial pace at which he seemed to be changing, and his propensity for stepping on people's toes, there was an unwritten agreement that it was best if he circled the church at a safe distance.

Therese had been wounded years earlier by a core member of the church. She wanted to leave, but her family liked it there, so to appease them she stayed and suffered in silence. The leadership member had been in the wrong, but his core buddies had protected him, allowing her to be scapegoated for their sinful actions. She was so trust-damaged that she couldn't imagine ever serving God in this place again, though she dreamed of serving him somehow, somewhere else, someday.

Bill and I liked the people such as Jeannie, Frank, John, Jerry, and Therese that we met at the church during the time we, as new people, were de facto members of the meteor belt. As we started answering "Help Wanted" ads successfully, we eventually got called on to become involved in leadership, serving the congregation as we orbited in the first ring out from the sun.

An odd and sadly unsurprising thing happened. Since serving the needs of the organization demanded so much of me, I became guarded about how I divvied up my limited free time and attention. Stepping back from some of those meteor belt relationships, I began to categorize the people who orbited out there as service projects, not human beings who needed a friend—just as Bill and I had when we first came to the church. I chose to let the gravitational pull of the sun, with its bright promise of a purposeful life, pull me toward it. After all, wasn't serving the church the highest, best way of serving God?

After several years of crazy-busy lives, we moved from the area. "What will we do without you?" the leadership asked rhetorically when we told them we were leaving. "You're such key players at our church."

Within a few months, it was as if we had never been there. Others were pulled from a lower orbit into a tighter one, netting them "promotions" in order to fill our positions. A half a handful of people from the church stayed in touch. But the rest of it, all of that busyness, all of that activity, passed into a season in our life that had been crammed with lots of friendly coworkers, but few friends.

So we're back in the meteor belt again, looking for a church home.

The loneliness I experienced during those five minutes after the end of the Sunday service when no one seemed to want to talk to us was a mix of sorrow and a gentle slap-in-the-face for me. The sorrow was rooted in both the grief of saying goodbye to our old life and the repentance that caused me to bid farewell to a piece of my ego that was bloated with my own importance. The slap-in-the-face was God's kind question: "Hey, you looking at me?" When I did, I knew he was asking me to tell him what I saw when I looked at the meteor belt this time around.

And what I discovered was that he was just as present in the meteor belt as I believed he was when I was circling the blazing sun. Maybe even more so. The people "out there" are just the kind of people who love to orbit near Jesus.

Those lonely five minutes at the end of the church service—and the quieter, saner pace of our lives—gave me the gift of time to consider my motivations for answering church bulletin "Help Wanted" ads in the future. I realized that my former church commitments had often come out of a place in me that was really hoping for a mailbox flooded with replies to my own private personal ad, one worded something like this:

Married Jewish Female Who Loves Jesus (MJFWLJ) in search of a friend.

God gently reminded me that I could be the kind of friend I longed for to those out here in the meteor belt. In the past, I'd been guilty of the sins of pragmatism and selfishness when I'd served my way into the inner orbit. This cleverly-disguised icky part of me valued position and politics just a little too much, and was willing to trade away friendship to gain something much shallower and less important.

Jesus was there in all 300 seconds of those lonely five minutes, loving me and inviting the now-exposed icky parts of me to friendship with him. As I've turned to him, he's begun to transform my need to be needed into a purer desire to serve. I get to be free to change poopy diapers in a church nursery or staff a food pantry or serve on a leadership team from a place of true authority—together with my new friends living at the edge of the solar system, which just so happens to be a gateway to eternity.

In Real Time

"I want what I have, and I want what you have, too."

I ran across this statement recently and it sums up the envy issue pretty well. "Wanting what you have, too" has been sadly true in my own life, whether it was my portion of the Twinkie my mom split so my sister and I could share it (Jodi got the bigger half—I know it) or whether it's been the promise of position or relationships.

What is it for you? Power? Money? Sex? Twinkies?

Most of us can taste the bile that rises in us when we're jealous. In the story that Jesus told about the generous boss, you can almost hear the sour grapes in the vineyard workers' question to their employer. "How is this fair? We've worked all day for the exact same pay as the guys who worked for you for an hour at most."

The vineyard owner's response is a reminder that in our bulls-and-bears world, God's economy will never make any sense to us as long as we want what we have, and what others have, too. The vineyard owner reminds the complainers that they agreed to the pay rate, telling them that what he agrees to pay others is not their concern. Then he identifies their real problem with this question: "Are you envious because I am generous?" (Mt 20:15).

Besides our own envy issues, this question also exposes what we believe about God's character. At some level, many of us struggle to believe that God is fair. If he were, then wouldn't he give me what he gave to someone else? Like maybe not just a perfectly divided Twinkie half, but the whole blooming Twinkie? We look at the Twinkie ... family ... friends ... job ... gifts ... he has given us, and conclude that he must love someone else more.

Consider a few of the things the Bible says about jealousy:

Jealousy can consume us:
" ... love is as strong as death, its jealousy unyielding as the grave. It burns like blazing fire, like a mighty flame" (Sg 8:6).

Jealousy drives our competition with others:
"And I saw that all labor and all achievement spring from man's envy of his neighbor. This too is meaningless, a chasing after the wind. The fool folds his hands and ruins himself. Better one handful with tranquility than two handfuls with toil and chasing after the wind" (Eccl 4:4–6).

Jealousy causes unholy divisions and classifications between people:
"You are still worldly. For since there is jealousy and quarreling among you, are you not worldly? Are you not acting like mere men? For when one says, "I follow Paul," and another, "I follow Apollos," are you not mere men? What, after all, is Apollos? And what is Paul? Only servants, through whom you came to believe—as the Lord has assigned to each his task" (1 Cor 3:3–5).

Our battle with the seeming unfairness of things comes from a place inside that isn't quite convinced that God is enough. We use a ruler and a scale to try to measure his immeasurable love and grace, and become immediately convinced that others are getting more than we. (Have you ever met someone who thought he'd received too much from

God? I haven't either.) By extension, we aren't convinced that our Twinkie is ever enough, either.

Psalm 73 is one songwriter's battle with envy. Spend some time listening to—or even singing—his words as he wrestles with jealousy over the seeming unfairness of things in his world before he is pinned in a half-nelson of surrender, worshiping God. We have been given a full day's pay, and we haven't earned a cent of it. A truthful song of surrender, sung over and over again, helps us remember that.

Continue the Conversation:
How would living the belief that the last will be first, and the first will be last, change the way that we relate to others in our lives? Can you think of examples?

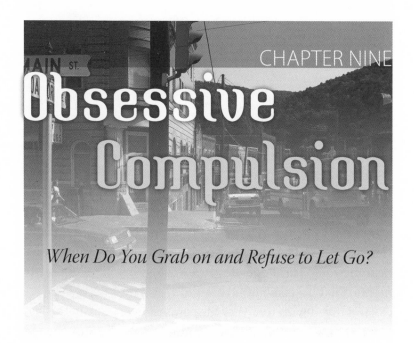

CHAPTER NINE

Obsessive Compulsion

When Do You Grab on and Refuse to Let Go?

A Woman with A One-Track Mind

Then Jesus told his disciples a parable to show them that they should always pray and not give up. He said: "In a certain town there was a judge who neither feared God nor cared about men. And there was a widow in that town who kept coming to him with the plea, 'Grant me justice against my adversary.'

"For some time he refused. But finally he said to himself, 'Even though I don't fear God or care about men, yet because this widow keeps bothering me, I will see that she gets justice, so that she won't eventually wear me out with her coming!'"

And the Lord said, "Listen to what the unjust judge says. And will not God bring about justice for his chosen ones, who cry out to him day and night? Will he keep putting them off? I tell you, he will see that they get justice, and quickly. However, when the Son of Man comes, will he find faith on the earth?"

—Luke 18:1–8

Reloaded: Get on My Case

"No matter where I go, there she is." He sighed and took another long pull of his drink. He was safe inside the dark, smoky inn, a Cheers-like place where everyone knew his name. It should have been off-limits for a lady like her.

His buddy had to yell above the din in the place. "Hey, you think she's a stalker? Maybe you could get a restraining order or something. Have one of your boys toss her in jail for a few nights. That'll shake her up a little."

He'd toyed with that very idea almost every day in the last few weeks, when he saw her standing there like Stonehenge outside his courtroom, waiting for him.

"Judge … may I please speak with you? It's about my case." Her soft voice and mousy appearance didn't command his attention—at first. In the culture of the time, she dressed the part of a poor young widow who knew she would probably never be asked to remarry. Her widowhood appeared to have left her with nothing. No family to turn to. No kids to take her in. Without a safety net, this meant that her career choices were as slim as her bank account appeared to be. She could support herself by begging. She could sell herself into slavery. Or she could become a hooker.

He'd learned over the past few weeks that a favorable decision in her court case would give her another option—financial independence. Most of her deceased husband's assets had been frozen by a business competitor who'd attempted a kind of ancient corporate takeover. His accountants and lawyers had frozen distribution of the estate under a mountain of complicated legal motions and requests for continuances that would keep the case tied up for years, if not decades. The guy had an army of legal talent working for him. The penniless widow had nothing except her conviction that if only a judge would scrutinize the case, he'd be able to unbury the truth. She was sure of it.

The judge took another long pull of his drink. "Nah, she's not a stalker. She doesn't want anything from me except for me to hear her case. I keep telling her she's got to wait her turn, but she says that her turn needs to be now."

It had been easy to ignore her at first. She'd stood unsmiling and somber outside of his courtroom every single day, calling out his name in a voice that was surprisingly childlike. It was a whisper in the cacophony of a busy courthouse complex.

"Please, sir … my case … ."

The first few times, he ignored her. He had no recollection of her specific case, or when she'd first made an appearance in his courtroom. A busy guy, he couldn't be expected to keep track of all of the shekel and dime civil cases that crossed his bench.

But he soon noticed that she was waiting for him outside of the courthouse every day. Every stinking day! "Sir, please. If you could just look at my case."

He tried ignoring her. He said polite things to her, hoping she'd leave him alone: "I'll have one of my assistants look into it next week, ma'am." He had no intention of actually doing this, but he thought maybe this would placate her. He even tried telling her to just run along home, and he'd get back to her as soon as he could. She looked at him with those sad brown eyes and said in a quiet voice, "I'd go home if I had one, sir. The case … ." He walked away before she could launch into her sorry story. Again.

She was right back in the same place the next day, waiting.

After a few weeks of this, he snapped and asked her for the case name and number. She said gravely, "Please don't hand this on to one of your assistants, sir. I'd really appreciate it if you'd personally review the case. I know if you look at the facts, you'll decide fairly."

He pulled the documents for the case after that, flipping through it quickly. The case was small potatoes compared to most that came before him. She'll get her hearing eventually, he thought. Her case will just have to work its way through the system. He tossed the file aside.

He decided to go back to his original plan of ignoring her, hoping she'd disappear until her day in court.

Shortly after that, she changed tactics. She was waiting outside the health club where he went twice a week for a steam and a massage. "Sir, did you get a chance to review my case?" She couldn't have been more out of place, looking for all the world like a fragile bone china tea cup someone had placed on the counter at McDonald's.

The mousy widow next showed up at his house, tagging along behind a man delivering packages to the address. She delivered a singing telegram in her flat, sad monotone. She swept the floor of the courtroom one morning, trying to catch his eye. She positioned herself next to the beggar he always passed each day on his way to work.

She even started appearing at the edges of his dreams, teary-eyed, always saying the same thing: "My case, my case."

The next morning, the widow was there waiting outside the courtroom. Again. After a night with her interrupting his dreams, it felt like he'd just spent eight hours with a broken record.

He pulled out her file, and called her to the bench. "You know, once this case comes to trial, it may not go your way."

She nodded gravely. "That's a risk I'm willing to take. I think that the facts will speak for themselves. I want justice to be done."

She stood there looking at him, unblinking. Waiting.

"If I cut through all the legal red tape your opponent has spun around this case, will you leave me alone?" he asked.

She burst into a huge smile and nodded yes.

He had never seen her smile before.

Bible scholar David Wenham explains that the word Jesus used to express the way the judge was worn out by the widow's persistence can literally be translated "giving me a black eye." Her insistence had a violent edge to it, leaving the judge feeling battered because she would not relent.

Jesus told the crowd following him at an earlier point in his ministry, "From the days of John the Baptist until now, the kingdom of heaven has been forcefully advancing, and forceful men lay hold of it" (Mt 11:12). He chose aggressive language to describe the kind of intense, single-minded pursuit of a completely different kingdom and King from any they had ever known.

The perfect image to capture this kind of pursuit? A grieving widow who has been wronged.

ParableLife: The Coach

My favorite thing to do? Sitting with a big cup of coffee—black, with sugar—and a friend or two, and talking. Laughing. Reading. Listening to music.

My second favorite thing to do? Having a refill. And maybe a biscotti. Or a macaroon. Some decent dark chocolate.

Ninety-fourth on my list of favorite activities is exercise. Though I'm sure that my negative childhood P.E. experiences have something to do with it, I've mostly chalked up my distaste for all things athletic to the sweat factor. When I sweat, it means that I'm going to have to find a blow dryer and round brush, stat. I have hair with the texture of rusty steel wool that requires a lot of maintenance in order to tame it. You know those pictures of people getting off the boat at Ellis Island at the turn of the twentieth century? A lot of them had kinky, frizzy hair. Some of those people were my relatives, and I'm telling you, their bad hair genes are industrial strength.

Anyway, it's always seemed to me that in order to exercise properly, you need to be able to pull your Jennifer Anniston hair back into a cute little scrunchie. When I get sweaty, my hair turns into a wire ball the size of a small meteoroid. Just try putting a scrunchie around that.

However, for exercise to have its intended effect, sweat is usually part of the formula. But in my head, the equation went something like "sweat + hair = another forty-five minutes after exercise undoing the damage to the do." I have better things to do, like drinking coffee and eating biscotti. Or organizing old files. Anything but exercise.

There is a cost to living this way. The principle of inertia had taken hold of me—you know, an object at rest tends to remain at rest—and the other principle that happens to objects at rest had gripped my body. Extra soft, wiggly pounds. After avoiding any kind of regular exercise for more than a decade, I wasn't too happy with how the extra biscotti weight and overall fatigue were making me feel. I decided I would give exercise another try at one of those half-hour workout joints. My hair and I would go exercise, and we'd get over ourselves.

Guess what? After a few weeks, once the novelty wore off, I discovered that I couldn't blame my exercise loathing solely on my wire hairball. No one at the gym seemed to care what my hair looked like. They never had. The truth was that I'd gotten lazy. I began finding reasons not to exercise: dry cleaning emergency! Urgent toilet cleaning crisis! I have to read the paper RIGHT NOW!

Gee. Maybe my exercise issues never had much to do with my hair after all.

I've discovered that there are quite a few of us out there who struggle with how to best take care of our bodies in a society that sends us schizophrenic messages about physical appearance. On one hand, we have surgically enhanced hotties parading across screens or telling us what beauty is from the cover of magazines. On the other hand, we are a SuperSize nation that has difficulty saying "no."

These dueling messages create some weird behaviors in people. I have a friend named Maggie who decided she didn't like the way she looked after her last baby was born, so she decided that she needed to train in order to run a marathon. She spent the summer running and running and running. She ate weird stuff. She ran some more. Her military discipline really impressed me. That fall, she finished the marathon— and hasn't run one since. Maggie had extracted what she wanted out of the experience (she lost thirty pounds and got the tee-shirt). She returned to the busy-ness of civilian life, and her summer experience evaporated as her runner's muscles melted away.

I have another friend named Paul who decided to start weight training a few years ago. He was just a regular guy who worked with computers, a modern-day Clark Kent.

But his body responded like it had been waiting for him to lift weights his whole life. He exploded, getting big, ripped muscles. The focus of his life became his body. When he plateaued after months of amazing physical transformation, a couple of the guys with whom he worked out offered him a surefire fix—steroids. Once he started juicing, Paul discovered a tantalizing shortcut to the body of his obsessive dreams.

Kim, another friend of mine, was a physical education major in college, and had a secret habit of binging on multiple pints of Ben and Jerry's and bags of potato chips at one o'clock in the morning. Her knowledge of human physiology and exercise came in handy in the middle of the night. After her binges, Kim would barf to get rid of the contents of her stomach. She followed her purge with a chaser of two hours of kick boxing at three a.m.

Though you'd think that my friends and I all have body issues, in actuality, none of these struggles is only about our external packaging. There is something broken inside of each of us that's responded to society's pressure to either be beautiful or to indulge ourselves, or both. My laziness has more to do with flabby character than frizzy hair. Maggie, Paul, and Kim each found ways to shortcut or avoid dealing with the broken places inside of them that are like petri dishes for lies: that a sprinter's mentality can be applied to the long-term run through life; that shortcuts are okay, that you can have it all.

Thanks to this exercise issue, not too long ago I had one of those light bulb moments about my life with God. Ever since I first felt the embrace of Jesus's forgiveness, I have wanted to learn to better communicate with him. I would pray grocery lists of needs; I'd pray Scripture, I'd journal, I'd listen in silence, and I'd release the language of praise that the Holy Spirit had placed inside of me, hands raised to heaven in surrender.

But mostly, I tend to be a slug, sitting around drinking coffee and eating biscotti, talking about God with people instead of talking to God. Once in a while, in a burst of energy, I've tried running a prayer marathon at a sprinter's pace. I've tried shortcuts (ask me about how many books about prayer I've read over the years, looking for the magic bullet). I've tried purging distractions and fat from my life, punishing myself for my weakness.

"Lord, teach me to pray," I'd say, sometimes too glibly, but meaning it. I really had no idea what I was asking for.

His answer was something along the lines of "OK."

God then sent a personal trainer to drag me out of my lethargy and earth-bound efforts. Elizabeth, a seventy-something immigrant who metaphorically dragged me off my spiritual can, handed me a do-rag for my hair, and said, "Forget the scrunchie. And the cookies. And the fake goals, shortcuts, and purges, as long as you're at it."

She was a towering older woman with rock star confidence who became my long distance ad hoc mentor. I first met Elizabeth at her son's wedding as we stood in line for the bathroom. We shared all of nine seconds of small talk before she zeroed in on me, her piercing dark eyes demanding truth, and asked me if I knew Jesus. It was like meeting a laser beam.

This was one intense woman. Have you ever met anyone like that—someone who could dive into deep, murky waters and immediately do water ballet with you? Well, we had quite a conversation right there in the bathroom line. I answered her question, "Yes, I know Jesus." But she heard the words I didn't speak, "I know him, but I wish I knew him better."

I'm not exactly sure how it happened after that, but Elizabeth and I swapped addresses and began a correspondence that continued over the next few years. She'd ask questions about my life, and I knew that she was praying for me. She'd occasionally call, always out of the clear blue, telling me that the Lord had placed me on her heart. She'd read a passage of Scripture and give me a shot of wisdom, straight up.

I learned about Elizabeth's life during our correspondence, too. She spent some of her days going to the nursing home to "minister to the old people," and other days she hung out with younger people, being their friend and listening to the stuff going on in their lives. Praying for all of them.

She told me that she was the child of parents who'd barely survived the Armenian genocide at the beginning of the twentieth century. The family had landed in the U.S. with nothing except their Orthodox Christian faith and the will to survive. After she was widowed as a young woman for the second (!) time, she experienced spiritual renewal at a Pentecostal church service. She was active in both churches, serving as a one-woman bridge between these two wildly diverse arms of the body of Christ.

Though she had learned the shape of the mystery of seeking God in the Orthodox liturgy, and the unstructured passion of seeking God through the language of worship, it took pain to braid these two strands of her life into a wick that God would light through prayer.

Along with the heartache of losing two husbands to illness, Elizabeth had watched helplessly as her youngest son David became addicted to drugs in his late teens. He transformed from a party man to a troubled man to a divorced husband and father to, finally, a homeless man.

David's saga had been going on for nearly twenty-five years when I met Elizabeth. Early on, she told me, she'd been too quick to bail him out, give him money or shelter. She also knew he was locked in grief over the death of his father, and she didn't know how to help him. She'd cycled through sadness, anger, self-recrimination, shortcuts, and countless interventions, an emotional merry-go-round of grief that parents of prodigals ride. The first few years, she watched helplessly as David couldn't disembark from his own ride, an addiction roller coaster of hopeful ups followed by plummeting slides downward. Over and over again, she begged God to do something—anything—to save her son from the clutches of evil and give him back to her.

Things just kept getting worse.

As her wait for David's return stretched into its first decade, she began to realize that too much of her prayer life was focused on seeking God for the gift of a restored son, and not because she hungered for the Giver. At one especially low point, when she was frantic because she didn't know where David was living or even if he was still alive, she heard God ask her, "Will you love me even if your son never returns to me?"

It wasn't an easy question to answer. The question forced her to admit that her one-woman army, bent on assaulting heaven to get her son released from hell, was the wrong paradigm for living her life with Jesus. David had become a kind of idol in her life. "You idolize what you fear," she told me. "I was full of fear about David's life and choices. He was a gift from God that had slowly become a point of obsession in my life."

She told God that *yes*, she'd love him even if David never came back to the Lord, or to her. This *yes* was the match that set the wick of her life on fire.

John Wesley, the preacher man in the 1700s who was not content to live his spiritual life as usual, had described his

God-hunger with the memorable words: "I set myself on fire and people come to watch me burn." Elizabeth's surrender to God meant that she was free to pursue him, reaching for him in everything she did. From hanging out at the nursing home, to being a friend to young people, to sitting in her apartment reading the paper, Elizabeth had allowed herself to be set on fire.

God gave me an opportunity to watch her burn when I visited Elizabeth in her hometown of San Francisco. I'd had the long-distance education tutorial on a life of prayer. Now I was getting the up-close-and-personal intensive experience. Elizabeth didn't have a recipe or a program that would teach me to live a life of prayer. She simply schlepped me around with her as she followed Jesus everywhere.

We prayed as we drove through Berkeley. We prayed as we sat in the sunshine at the Golden Gate Bridge. We prayed as we ate lunch, as we walked, as we sat in her living room talking. We prayed for David, for the rest of her family, for my family, for the people we saw that day, for people we didn't know, for our churches. Lacing our intercessions together was a constant thread of worship. God, you are good! You are faithful! You are beautiful, pure, and just!

Was she a religious addict? Obsessed? Unbalanced? If she was, she was the healthiest, most vibrant, mentally ill person I'd ever met. She was fearless about coming to her faithful, just Lord. Everywhere, all the time, she trusted him with the injustices in her world.

Intercessors aren't born, she told me. They're made, choice by choice, by people who have no other options but to follow Jesus everywhere. People who live a life of prayer are completely convinced that they are helpless to bring freedom and justice to the people and situations in their lives. So they depend on the only one who can. And does. And will.

Elizabeth made me shuck my excuses, shortcuts, and purge-like promises to try harder just in time for a long stretch of difficult road in my life and marriage that included a failed adoption, the death of my dad, a tough relocation, the challenges of helping our kids navigate their teen years, and a church split.

My own well honed tendencies toward slacker behavior ("Coffee, anyone?") and rational-sounding avoidance excuses ("Toilet cleaning crisis!") bubbled to the surface during this time in my life. I often cried out for the gift of a quick fix and a happy ending. Elizabeth reminded me sweetly that I was asking for the wrong gift.

If God hadn't placed Elizabeth in my life, I might never have suspected that this hard stuff was a summons to exercise my faith, seeking God with the commitment of a Marine drill sergeant and the passion of a young lover.

I'm learning that it is. And I am.

In Real Time

Don't you think it's an interesting choice that Jesus picked an unfair judge who claims not to fear God or man to be the hinge of the parable at the beginning of this chapter? It's funny how the judge ends up responding in a kind of wearied fear to the "assaults" of the powerless but persistent widow.

Jesus then attaches another hinge to the story when he contrasts this earthbound judge with God. If justice can be extracted from a worldly guy like the judge, Jesus says, then God's friends can be sure that justice is a certainty for them: "And will not God bring about justice for his chosen ones, who cry out to him day and night? Will he keep putting them off? I tell you, he will see that they get justice, and quickly.

However, when the Son of Man comes, will he find faith on the earth?" (Lk 18:7–8).

There's so much unfairness at work in the world. There are garden variety injustices: schoolyard bullies who terrorize the weak, nepotism, cheating on tests. There's SuperSize injustice: war, racism, genocide, murder. Evil.

Injustice large or small has the potential to destroy our faith in God. If we apply our own standard to the handling of it, we quickly lose hope in his ability to judge evil fairly and triumph over it in the end. But, Jesus tells us that he'll find true faith in those who've pursued him in prayer because they live convinced that only he can and will set things right. This kind of prayer says, "Lord, I trust you to do what your Word says you will. I'm choosing to refrain from taking matters into my own hands. I'm choosing to refrain from revenge. I am waiting on you, trusting your character. I am hungry to see your completely just love triumph."

In our world, this kind of persistent prayer rises from prison cells in China. From refugee camps in Somalia. From orphanages in Romania. From small apartments in San Francisco.

From coffee shops.

From you. And me.

(You might be interested to know that Elizabeth's son David returned to God after nearly twenty-five years of addiction. You might also be interested, but not surprised, to learn that this development didn't change a single thing about the way she continued to live her life before God.)

Take a few minutes in a quiet place to listen to another story Jesus told to his disciples about relentlessly seeking God even when the answers don't come quickly and justice seems a long way off:

Then he said, "Imagine what would happen if you went to a friend in the middle of the night and said, 'Friend, lend me three loaves of bread. An old friend traveling through just showed up, and I don't have a thing on hand.'

"The friend answers from his bed, 'Don't bother me. The door's locked; my children are all down for the night; I can't get up to give you anything.'

"But let me tell you, even if he won't get up because he's a friend, if you stand your ground, knocking and waking all the neighbors, he'll finally get up and get you whatever you need.

"Here's what I'm saying: Ask and you'll get; seek and you'll find; knock and the door will open."

—Luke 11:5–9 (*The Message*)

Asking, seeking, and knocking aren't things we do only once and then give up. They are verbs of relentless persistence that shape not only the way we must pray, but the choices we make about how we spend our days. We are inflamed to pursue God as if our very lives depend on it.

Continue the Conversation:
In what area of your life have you given up or lost faith? What circumstances or beliefs have caused you to stop asking, seeking, knocking … persisting? Why? What would it take to begin again?

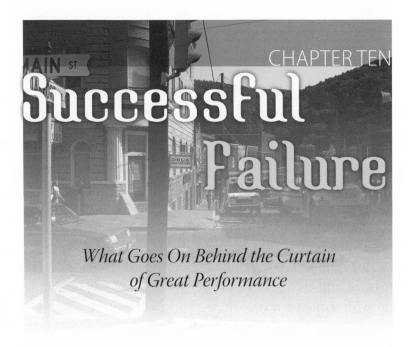

CHAPTER TEN

Successful Failure

*What Goes On Behind the Curtain
of Great Performance*

A Religious Superstar and a Religious Flop

> To some who were confident of their own righteousness
> and looked down on everybody else, Jesus told this
> parable: "Two men went up to the temple to pray, one a
> Pharisee and the other a tax collector. The Pharisee stood
> up and prayed about himself: 'God, I thank you that I am
> not like other men—robbers, evildoers, adulterers—or
> even like this tax collector. I fast twice a week and give a
> tenth of all I get.'
>
> "But the tax collector stood at a distance. He would
> not even look up to heaven, but beat his breast and said,
> 'God, have mercy on me, a sinner.'"
>
> —LUKE 18:9–14

Reloaded: Watch the Show with the Sound Turned Down

There's an amazing dance in this story, but it's really easy to miss the choreography because the music of these words is so dissonant. Mute the words for a few moments, and watch the movement of the men.

The first man comes into view, walking tentatively into a large, welcoming courtyard, each step full of exquisite pain. The closer he gets to his destination, the harder it becomes for him to walk. The invisible weight on his shoulders grows heavier with each step. He pauses for a moment, then forces himself forward a few steps more. As he does, the tears he's been fighting to hold inside spill down his face.

He begins to sob and can move no farther. His hands cover his face, and his body shakes uncontrollably. When his hands drop for a moment, you can see his lips moving. It's like he's shouting, even while he's bent over. He reaches out as if to grab a lifeline, and then, as he looks at his outstretched hand, he weeps anew. And in a sudden, stabbing movement, he balls his hand into a fist and brings it sharply into his chest. The movement brings a fresh wave of tears, and he repeats the motion again and again—left fist, right fist, left fist. It is an action typically reserved for women mourners of his culture, a physical response to a broken, grief-torn heart.

Others in the busy courtyard stare, then try not to stare. The man's grief is an intimacy that is difficult for most of the crowd to watch for more than a moment. There are clusters of people pretending that his hemorrhage of pain is not happening.

But one man, standing at front of the courtyard, back to the crowd, can't ignore him. The spotlight is not on him, and alpha man doesn't like it one bit. Those standing near Mr. Alpha have formed an impromptu amphitheater around him.

When he glances over his shoulder at the disruption, a look of annoyance flickers across his face. He takes a deep breath, marshalling all of his formidable energy into recapturing what he believes belongs to him.

Mr. Alpha repositions himself, throwing his shoulders back as if he's giving a speech. His face tilts upwards, hands cupped upwards just so. Reenergized by the competition, he continues his oration. But the other man's cries, echoing from the far corner of the courtyard, are impossible to ignore.

In a final attempt to regain the crowd, the spotlight, Mr. Alpha whirls around. His eyes flash rage, but his face is a mask of calm. He is a professional, after all, and is used to being a klieg light at a Hollywood premiere. Mr. Alpha flicks his wrist like he's aiming a cannon at the weeping man, firing a dismissive gesture toward him. He then turns his back to the crowd once again. Payoff: They're all looking at him.

Everyone, that is, except for the weeping man.

Turn the sound up and listen.

ParableLife: Fence

She had dug another hole.

Then she'd hoisted the splintery fence post and dropped it into the empty hollow. There was a satisfying thud as it hit bottom. She leveled the post expertly and poured quick-set concrete around it.

She stepped back to admire her work. Lined up like a marching band in formation, her rectangular fence line contained everything she cared about. Each fence post was a sentry standing guard at the perimeter of her property, an immovable promise of security.

The fence was certain to keep them all safe.

Here's a story about the fence. The names are disguised, but the guts of the story are true.

Lynne glanced across the church at Brian and Cindy Jennis. Weird to see Amber sitting with them. That kid hadn't been in church in months. Brian and Cindy were sitting there, backs rod-straight, not looking to the right or the left. Amber was hunched over, her filthy coat wrapped around her like a shield. She was completely absorbed with examining her split ends.

At least it's winter, Lynne thought. *She has to cover up now. It's way too cold outside for us all to be treated to the Amber Show at this time of year.*

Though it seemed like about three-quarters of the youth group girls dressed provocatively, Lynne was sure that one hundred percent of the girls who didn't come to youth group but got dragged to church by their parents dressed like they were auditioning for one of those trashy music videos. For probably the 2,479th time, Lynne's thoughts circled the same groove around her heart: *Do we really have to look at everyone's cleavage and bra straps and bellies when we're supposed to be worshiping God?* Amber had been one of the worst offenders before she stopped coming to church a year ago.

She'd felt a smug, warm pity for Brian and Cindy, going through whatever it was they were going through with Amber. They seemed like such nice people, but clearly they were powerless to exert any control over that daughter of theirs.

She used to be a pretty good kid, but then those teen hormones hit like a hurricane. Amber used to be one of Lynne's regular babysitters, and she had thought of her as a sweet, reliable girl. She'd even recommended Amber as a babysitter to the new associate pastor's wife.

Once Amber hit high school, she seemed hellbent on flushing all of her good morals down the commode like she had a case of spiritual diarrhea. Amber started dressing like a tramp, and Lynne's oldest daughter, Bethany, reported that her favorite babysitter mostly talked on the phone with boys instead of fulfilling her duties. Some time after that, a boy came over to see Amber while she was babysitting after all the little ones were asleep. Bethany, who had gotten up for a drink of water, discovered the visitor lounging on the living room couch eating some potato chips. That was the end of Amber's babysitting career at their house.

"Over there, Mommy. Is that Amber?" Eight-year old Bethany whispered.

"Yeah, honey, it is." Lynne tried to sound disinterested.

Bethany whipped her head around and waved at Amber. Amber gave her a small crooked smile, then went back to counting her split ends.

"Bethany, don't stare."

Ignoring her, Bethany said a little too loudly, "She looks different."

That was an understatement, Lynne thought. Amber looked like an iron shell of her old self: dark eyes in a white face; too-short, too-red hair; garnishes of silver rimming her ear cartilage and slashing through one eyebrow.

"Well, it's good to see her back in church," Lynne replied. She knew what the right words were, and said them. But her disapproving tone drained those just-right words of meaning.

The tone was the sonic equivalent of a post-hole digger, excavating a spot for another boundary marker on the perimeter of Lynne's family. Disapproval. Bethany, you must never be like Amber. She's bad. Very, very bad.

Lynne would finish the job in the car after church, dropping some words into this new hole until a rule took shape. "Young ladies need to be modest," Lynne began.

Thankfully, Dan took the cue, giving their four kids a brief speech about appropriate dress for Christians before they left the parking lot and headed home for lunch and for the blessed relief of one fenced piece of heaven in this crazy, unsafe world.

A few weeks later, Lynne heard through the grapevine that Amber was pregnant. Of course she was, Lynne thought. Anyone could see that the girl was out of control.

If only Brian and Cindy had stricter rules and stuck by their guns about them, Lynne thought. *No kid of mine would ever leave the house looking like Amber, no way. She picked up that rebellious stuff at public school. And she picked up a whole lot more, too.*

Lynne and Dan weren't going to make those mistakes, nosiree. They'd fortressed their family with rules, one fence post at a time, and strung barbed wire of sour words between the fence posts, an insurance policy meant to keep the kids inside their safety zone at all times:

"We don't listen to that worldly music in this house."

"You can invite the kids in the neighborhood to come to church with us, but I don't want you over at their homes. They don't come from Christian families, and who knows what they watch on the TV over there."

"I don't want you looking like a tramp. Dress like a Christian young lady would."

"We don't watch movies like that."

"Would Jesus do that?"

"No."

"No."

"No."

"We have to live in the world, but we're not of the world."

And then, just for some variety:

"No."

Twelve years later, the barbed wire running between the fence post rules along the perimeter of Lynne's family had rusted away, and four or five of the fence posts running along the west edge of the family had been toppled. It took sledgehammer force to topple posts set in concrete, but that's just what Bethany had done before she escaped the fortress a few weeks after she turned eighteen.

The purple-gray light of late afternoon in late January afternoon soaked the air with the kind of sadness that you could almost wring out and drink. *Wonder where she is today,* Lynne thought. She absently pulled ingredients out of the fridge for dinner. Bethany gone, eighteen-year-old Anna away at college, the family was shrinking even as the borders had been left sentryless.

So far, so good with Anna. Too soon to tell with the two younger boys. But hard to tell with any of them. After all, Bethany had maintained an outward compliance to the rules far longer than her heart had. Dan found a stack of her journals she'd left behind after she'd thrown her clothes in a duffle bag and backpack, jumped into a friend's car, and driven into what she expected would be a rule-free future. No fences. No barbed wire.

The journals detailed Bethany's rage at all their rules. They'd seen the rage emerge when she was sixteen. As they read, they learned that it had been simmering in her far longer than that. While she seemed outwardly compliant, going to youth group, dressing modestly, staying on the right side of the fence—a perfect little Pharisee—there was a girl-woman they didn't know who'd been pushing on the wires strung between the posts for years, dying to be free.

They could almost understand those feelings, but what they couldn't understand was the potency of Bethany's hunger for love.

Couldn't she see that those fence posts were a sign of their love for her? The rules were meant to protect, not hurt. The world out there was a dangerous place, and they wanted to make sure she wouldn't be damaged by it. They also wanted to guarantee that the people who mattered most to them in the world besides their family—church people—would respect them. They were a good Christian family. This fenced life was how good Christian families lived.

Right?

Now she didn't know where Bethany was sleeping at night, or where she was working. Oh, Bethany would call occasionally to touch base, but she kept tight-lipped about much of the details of her life. Bethany had erected a fence around her own new life that was designed to keep her parents out.

The phone rang as Lynne was chopping vegetables for stir-fry.

"Hi mom. It's me, Bethany."

Lynne's heart skipped a beat. It did every time she heard that voice on the other end of the phone.

Bethany took a breath. "Uh ... yeah. I was wondering if

you and Dad were going to be home tonight. I wanted to stop by and see you."

"Of course, honey," Lynne said. For one second, the thought flitted through Lynne's heart that maybe Bethany wanted to come home. "Did you want to join us for dinner?"

There was a pause. "No, thanks," Bethany said. "I can't. I'll be by about eight." Another pause. "Thanks for asking, though."

The moment the call ended, Lynne knew. Bethany was pregnant.

First thought: *She wouldn't be telling us if she wasn't intending to have the baby.*

Second thought: *I wonder who the father is.*

Third thought: *The Jennises.*

She hadn't thought about them in years. They'd moved out of the area not long after Amber had her baby. Lynne had heard that Amber had turned her life around, eventually marrying a youth pastor and having two other kids.

But it wasn't Amber Jennis she thought about now. It was Amber's parents, Brian and Cindy.

She walked into the bathroom to splash water on her face, her mind whirling. The memory of that morning at church twelve years ago suddenly came flooding back. She had not studied Brian and Cindy's faces that morning when what must have been a newly pregnant Amber came to church with them. She'd been too busy watching Amber like a hawk.

Though Brian and Cindy had been at the gauzy edges of her memory of that morning, suddenly it was as if Lynne shifted her gaze and brought their faces into sharp focus for the first time. In the mirror she could see their faces just as clearly as she saw her own.

The look of pain, shock, and confusion was identical.

Lynne's tears came like sudden hard rain. They came from an untouched reservoir inside of her, a place she'd entombed with her legalism and certainty.

These weren't the tears she'd cried while her relationship with Bethany was disintegrating, or the tears she'd cried when Bethany moved out, or even the tears she'd cried when she read those journals. Those tears were the tears of grief and loss.

Kneeling on the bathroom floor, holding her stomach as she sobbed great retching sobs, Lynne wept because she saw herself as she really was. She had spent years focusing on the consequences of everyone else's real and imagined transgressions. No matter how many times she heard that she was one at church, she had never seen herself as a sinner.

Her sin had enthusiastically evicted the Jennises from her fenced life, along with dozens of other she'd judged unworthy over the years. Her sin had erected the fence in the first place. Her sin had masqueraded as righteousness but was nothing more than a lust for control. That lust was more dangerous than anything she could have kept out of her life.

Yeah. It was all sin. Lynne was a sinner.

Kneeling on the cold bathroom floor like a beggar, she told Jesus so.

Jesus loves sinners. Not fences.

And he told Lynne so.

In Real Time

There's Oscar and Emmy and Tony and their black sheep cousin Razzie, along with myriad other prizes for best stage or screen performance in a given year. But the way that many of us perform religion, you might be tempted to believe that there was a prize for "Superstar Christian Of The Month," maybe a statuette of some golden praying hands that look suspiciously like clapping hands. Let's call it the "Handy."

Even the media have noticed contemporary Christianity's preoccupation with religious performance. In recent years, we've seen Dana Carvey's late 1980s *Saturday Night Live* character "The Church Lady," Homer Simpson's annoying neighbor Ned Flanders, and Hilary Faye, the sweet-faced uber-Pharisee in the movie *Saved*.

Any of those characters would be thrilled to get their own Handy. They'd give an appropriately humble acceptance speech, while believing that they not only earned their Handy, they deserved it.

The rest of us laugh at these over-the-top caricatures, but see others we've known in them: We are suffocated by the ridiculous smallness of the Church Lady's soul. We roll our eyes at Ned's weird pronouncements about sin and righteousness, and cheer Homer's sarcastic responses. We cringe knowingly at Hilary Faye's gossipy prayer meetings and mean antics.

The people who've created these caricatures know a thing or two about the damage that religious acting can do. But real life religious performance is usually a more toxic and subtle version of Church Lady, Ned, or Hilary Faye. Consider these examples:

> The child driven to memorize Bible verses so he can compete against other driven children to win a prize at church. The church has told him that the prize will be a plaque, or even a trip to camp (where he'll memorize more Bible verses). But the real prize is the approval from the adults who represent Christ to him.

The painfully shy teen girl who has heard over and over again that if she were a superstar Christian people would be magnetically drawn to Jesus-in-her. Her face has just broken out in a fresh crop of acne, and she's a little overweight … at least for now. She's just discovered laxatives and thinks that maybe if she looks thinner, she'll be prettier and people will be attracted to her.

The guitarist who plays on his church's worship team every Sunday, is continually affirmed by people who tell him what a gift he has. If only they knew that he wasn't even sure he believed in God anymore. He likes the strokes he gets at the church, so he keeps his unbelief to himself while he leads the congregation in the worship of a God who seems like a fiction to him.

The 42-year-old woman whose second home is the church. She plans the Bible study, runs the nursery, organizes Vacation Bible School. She keeps the church activity program gears humming. Everyone knows that she's indispensable!

Every thing these people do has value: memorizing verses, living a spiritually attractive life, worshipping God, creating and participating in activities that help others grow in their faith. But when they do these things for the applause of an audience, these tasks are sapped of all value except that which the audience gives their work.

That audience is a tough crowd. Think unsmiling Olympic judges bent on hunting for flaws in the performance. Their applause is no louder than the polite approval you hear from the crowd at a golf tournament—if they applaud at all.

The sad thing is that religious performers paste God's name on the audience and say they're doing their show for him. But the whole notion is a sham, and it was shattered at Calvary. There isn't a one of us who could ever perform well enough for the one true God. He gave his children the Old Testament Law to show us not only what his character was like, but to let them know how they could stay connected to him in relationship. In turn, they spent generations either not doing what he asked, or turning the whole thing into a show.

He never wanted either of those things from them—or from any of us. He simply wanted our hearts fully engaged toward him. In his love, God embraced the rebels, and he offered performers a way to step off the stage. Jesus told the story of the religious superstar and the religious flop precisely because he values our genuine, risky brokenness, not our bland, safe production values.

In the first century, there was a Christian community in a place called Laodicea (located in modern Turkey). This church had become bland and stagnant. John, Jesus's beloved friend, experiences a supernatural interruption in the form of a series of visions at the end of his life. One slice of this vision includes the risen Christ speaking to the angel responsible for caring for the Laodicean church. John captures these words for them and for us: "I know your deeds, that you are neither cold nor hot. I wish you were either one or the other! So, because you are lukewarm—neither hot nor cold—I am about to spit you out of my mouth. You say, 'I am rich; I have acquired wealth and do not need a thing.' But you do not realize that you are wretched, pitiful, poor, blind and naked" (Rv 3:15–17).

Though this church had likely embraced financial security and stopped caring about everyone except themselves, there is a phrase in verse 17 that is at the core of all religious performance: "I ... do not need a thing." The religious professional in Jesus's story in Luke 18 did not need a thing. He was so full of the wealth of his good deeds and clean living that all he could do was live on stage, listening for the applause of men. Like Hans Christian Andersen's fairy tale emperor who paraded before his subjects in the buff, convinced he was wearing a beautiful new suit, the religious professional had convinced himself that he was dressed for spiritual success.

He tells the Laodiceans—and all of us who live like the religious thespian, acting like we need nothing from God except to see ourselves standing center stage—that we are "wretched, pitiful, poor, blind, and naked." The words apply to our friend the Pharisee, the proud religious professional in Jesus's story in Luke 18.

The religious failure in Jesus's story, the one who beat his breast and cried out for God's mercy, ran off whatever stage he commanded earlier in his life and into God's heart. He knew he was wretched, pitiful, poor, blind, and naked.

Wretched, pitiful, poor, blind, and naked.

Those adjectives were true of the man in the story, and they are true of me. You too?

The message to the Laodicean church offers everyone who knows the truth about themselves a gracious way off the stage: "I counsel you to buy from me gold refined in the fire, so you can become rich; and white clothes to wear, so you can cover your shameful nakedness; and salve to put on your eyes, so you can see. Those whom I love I rebuke and discipline. So be earnest, and repent. Here I am! I stand at the door and knock.

If anyone hears my voice and opens the door, I will come in and eat with him, and he with me" (Rv 3:18–20).

He tells all of us who have been trapped or burned by the quest for religious professionalism that he longs to …

… refine us, burning away the faux riches of adulation.

… clothe us, giving us true, beautiful garments instead of invisible, shameful costumes.

… heal us, so that we can see him and ourselves as we truly are.

… welcome us, not as a celebrity, but as a friend.

What he is asking us to do is walk off the stage. He wants to simply be with us, now. And in the end, he offers us that same relationship for eternity: "To him who overcomes, I will give the right to sit with me on my throne, just as I overcame and sat down with my Father on his throne" (Rv 3:21).

The first step in walking offstage is choosing to listen in silence to his Word without excuses or rationalization. Reread the story of the religious superstar and the religious flop (Lk 18:9–14) and the letter to the Laodicean church (Rv 3:14–22). Asking God to show you the ways you've bought into the performance lie. Listen. You'll be amazed at what he wants to say to you.

Continue the Conversation:

How have you been trapped by a need to engage in religious performance? How have you been burned by the religious performance of others?

CHAPTER ELEVEN

Unforced Slavery

Living as a Lover, Not an Employee

Commitment in Word Only

At that time the kingdom of heaven will be like ten virgins who took their lamps and went out to meet the bridegroom. Five of them were foolish and five were wise. The foolish ones took their lamps but did not take any oil with them. The wise, however, took oil in jars along with their lamps. The bridegroom was a long time in coming, and they all became drowsy and fell asleep.

At midnight the cry rang out: "Here's the bridegroom! Come out to meet him!"

Then all the virgins woke up and trimmed their lamps. The foolish ones said to the wise, "Give us some of your oil; our lamps are going out."

"No," they replied, "there may not be enough for both us and you. Instead, go to those who sell oil and buy some for yourselves."

But while they were on their way to buy the oil, the bridegroom arrived. The virgins who were ready went in with him to the wedding banquet. And the door was shut.

Later the others also came. "Sir! Sir!" they said. "Open the door for us!"

But he replied, "I tell you the truth, I don't know you."

Therefore keep watch, because you do not know the day or the hour.

— Matthew 25:1–13

Reloaded: Night Light

We stand in line behind the person with seventeen items (including one obscure item that needs a price check) in the "10 items or less" line at the grocery store. We sit in the doctor's office with a collection of coughing people, waiting to see the doctor. We queue up at ballpark bathrooms between innings. We pace the floor at two in the morning, listening for the sound of a car door that finally signals the arrival of a teen who should have been home hours earlier.

We wait to hear if we got the job. We wait for the show to begin. We wait for spouses and babies and celebration. We wait for change. We wait for God.

Jesus wanted his followers to learn how to wait when waiting would be painful, terrifying, and nearly impossible. This wait would expose those who followed him out of convenience, because it was socially acceptable, or because they were trained religious professionals.

Matthew 24 is a blunt, detailed description of this wait. Jesus told his followers that all the usual religious structures would be destroyed. False saviors would con people, including the biggest one of them all, a fake Messiah. Jesus reminds them that the Old Testament prophet Daniel could see the Big Fake positioned on the horizon of time. The world would convulse in birth pangs of real and rumored war, famine and earthquake. God's righteousness would be exercised in a world that he loved—a world that had chosen to scorn his love.

Jesus wanted his followers to know that there wouldn't be any rest stops on this superhighway heading toward the rebel world's final destination. There would be no place to refuel. The ones who will survive this trip are the ones who gas up, buckle their seatbelts, and choose not to believe any of the billboards promising a scenic alternate route.

To help his hearers understand the implications of Matthew 24, Jesus introduces us to a group of sweet girls chosen to be bridesmaids. In Jesus's day, bridesmaids weren't supposed to show up on the day of the wedding in matching dresses and line up like schoolchildren for pictures. They had real work to do as part of the preparation for the wedding day.

They were supposed to wait for the bridegroom, who could show up ready to meet his bride at any odd hour, day or night. Some grooms traveled to meet their bride from far distances. Other grooms had to spend time working through the financial arrangements of the marriage with their future in-laws before the ceremonies could take place. The bridesmaids' big assignment was to be there for the groom's arrival—even if it was two in the morning—and bring him to the bride. To prepare for a nighttime arrival, the bridesmaids needed to plan ahead so they'd have a stash of precious oil ready to light the journey and the start of the celebration.

A bridesmaid's wait was intensified, perhaps, by her own longing to be married someday. Thus, the wait for the bridegroom was charged with hopeful anticipation.

Doing the slacker minimum would not be enough. Jesus's parable ends with half the bridesmaids missing the party because they neglected to prepare. The unready bridesmaids may have had the bare minimum of oil for a regular day's work, but they didn't have enough to carry them through to the celebration. The foolish choices these unready bridesmaids made showed everyone that these girls really didn't understand what it meant to wait for the groom.

A wise pastor friend of mine says that lovers will do what workers can't. Those who clock in for a regular day's religious duty will not be prepared to wait for God through the writhing birth pangs of a dying world. Those who live as lovers of the Bridegroom can, and will.

ParableLife: Reconnecting

I have two friends named Angie and Jessica who were once a part of the same college fellowship, and both were committed, passionate followers of Jesus.

As they entered post-college adult life, they ended up in different corners of the country. They got busy living their lives in their new zip codes and lost touch with one another. But not too long ago, they had an opportunity to reconnect through—of all things—the upcoming wedding of another college friend named Jen.

Angie and Jessica began e-mailing one another in advance of Jen's big day, and they discovered that more had changed than just their respective zip codes.

Dear Angie—

I was really surprised to hear from you after all this time. Yes, of course, I'd love to see you when you're in town for Jen's wedding next month. I was invited, but I'm not going. I used to hang around with her a lot right after we graduated since we both ended up in the same city, but she and I have really gone different directions in our lives. She didn't have a problem letting me know that she disagreed with my choices.

I bet Jen doesn't even know that I moved out of Nate's place over a year ago and moved in with Jeff, a guy I met at a party last Christmas. We clicked right away and have been inseparable ever since. He's a website designer and makes really good money. He's a huge improvement over Nate, who was a bartender when he felt like it and happy to sponge off me when he didn't.

It seems like a million years ago since we were all in college, doesn't it? It'll be great to see you and get caught up on our lives in person. I'm working at a mid-sized law firm that handles immigration issues in the city, and studying to be a paralegal. What other career could you have imagined for an art major? Believe it or not, I'm really enjoying it. I used to hate research, remember? Now I can see how my research helps people and makes their lives more beautiful. That's a kind of art, too.

Who else do you stay in touch with from college? I feel like I've fallen off the edge of the world since those days. I haven't stayed in touch with anyone.

Jen's harsh take on my life kind of scared me off from making the attempt to connect with anyone else from our campus fellowship group. Maybe I shouldn't really blame her. After all, I made the decision to go a different direction, and now I just don't have much in common with most of those people anymore.

Your willingness to try to contact me (again) after all this time made me realize that maybe I was being too harsh, shutting off those years like they never happened. I am who I am, and I'm more at peace with myself now than I was a while ago. So I'm looking forward to seeing you and reminiscing a little.

Write when you have a chance and give me the headlines about your life since college. Let me know, too, what your schedule will be for the weekend of the wedding.

Jessica

Hey Jessica—
Thanks for getting back to me so quickly. I'm looking forward to visiting you, and of course, I'm really excited to see Jenny get married. Her fiancé is a great guy. I got a chance to spend some time with them about six months ago when they were headed out to the coast so she could meet his parents.

She and I talk about once a month, and all she's told me is that she's lost touch with you over the last couple of years. She just said that you'd kind of disconnected from God somehow, and asked me to pray for you. She didn't say much more than that. Remember how militant she was against gossip? She still is, which is why I didn't know much more than just those bare-bones facts.

It's amazing how much has changed in our lives since college, but I always imagined we'd all stay friends. When I think back to those years, it felt like we'd been through everything together. I realize how much we helped each other grow, and grow up.

You asked for the headlines about my life. You probably won't be surprised to learn that I'm a 5th grade teacher. The kids are so great—10- and 11-year olds are hanging between childhood and early adolescence, but are still mostly children when they're in 5th grade. They make every day different, which is great for a big kid like me.

The kids I taught my first year out of college are in high school now. Not too long ago, a girl from the class I'd taught my first year out of college—those poor guinea pigs!—came to see me and tell me how much I'd impacted her life. Those moments are why I love teaching. And yeah, the summers off are a great bonus!

I'm really involved in my church, and I teach 5th grade Sunday School there. I guess I can't get away from that age group! Working with the kids there is different because instead of having them write reports about famous scientists or learn about the geography of North America, I get to share Jesus with them.

It's funny— don't really use my teacher skills all that much in the classroom at my church. What I do use are the things I learned with people like you, Jen, and some of the others in our campus fellowship about following

Jesus in each moment of our lives. Even though we were there at school to study things like business (Jenny), education (me), and art (you), when I think about it, we really sort of lived through a kind of a seminary of real life there.

That "seminary" really helped when I ended up getting a job three-quarters of the way across the country after graduation. I didn't know a single person when I first got here. We learned in college to sink our roots deep into Jesus, and that deep root system carried me even through some pretty lonely times.

You'd asked who else I stay in touch with besides Jen. I still hear from Mark, Julio (he and his wife are now the proud parents of a brand new baby boy), Ming, and Sarah. They're all planning to come to the wedding. I really wish you'd reconsider and come, too. I know they'd all be glad to see you.

In Him,
Angie

Hey back, Angie—
No offense, but I don't think I can handle seeing all those people in one place again. It feels like I was another person back then, and when I think about those days, I barely recognize myself. You may not recognize me, either! My hair is plain old brown—not the strawberry pink and orange hair I had during our junior year.

I'm kind of surprised that you didn't mention anything about me living with Jeff. I still think of us back then as these really black-and-white, holier-than-thou chicks. If you would have told me then that I'd have drifted away from that brand of Christianity, I'd have told you that harmonicas could fly.

Who decides what's right and what's wrong? Certainly not me anymore. After I left the womb of college and got born into the real world, I discovered that Christianity was a lot more narrow and two dimensional than the 3-D world I had to figure out how to live in.

Finding a job that used my degree was impossible. I had rent to pay, my roommate moved out, and I went from a sophisticated art student with a great portfolio to a Starbucks employee in three months flat. When I think about that period of my life, it feels like a big dark hallway lined with locked doors. I was walking down the hallway, pounding on every door, and all of them stayed shut.

I felt that the God we used to talk so much about in college was the one holding all the doors shut. Everyone says that city life is so hip and glamorous, and it can be if you have money and friends, but it ain't very glamorous when you're a broke little Christian girl with a useless art degree.

When I first started working at Starbucks, a couple of my coworkers would invite me out to clubs to party with them. I got tired of sitting at home alone with bad furniture and an empty fridge, so I started hanging out with them. Before I knew it, I'd shed all those restrictive rules we wore in college like I was shedding skin that was too tight.

Christianity didn't work for me. There. I said it. You sure you still want to hang out with me (no lectures) even though I'm a pretty much a pagan these days?

Jessica

Hey Jessica—
I'm really glad you told me your story. I can understand some of what you went through because I found it bewildering to try to figure out how to build a grown-up life after college, too. It was really lonely here in a new town.

I looked for a church home, and the search made me feel even lonelier. There weren't many young adults at most of the churches I visited—just a lot of families and programs and activities, and I couldn't figure out where I fit in. I hated the way Sunday mornings felt, and it made the rest of the week feel pretty lousy, too.

I'd learned while we were in college that the hard times were when I really needed to lean hard on the Lord. I knew the 411, but doing it all alone was a whole other thing. It felt like I was using a toothpick to drill for oil through solid rock. I get it now that at least some of those emotions came from the grief I was experiencing over the drastic changes that had taken place in my life. There were these little moments of grace when I realized that he was there and that the lessons in trust we learned in college were true, so I hung on.

Right after I'd finally found a church I liked, I met Ron there. He was a wonderful guy, and we spent tons of time together. I even wondered if he might be "the one." After about six months of dating, I discovered he wasn't. We simply had different goals for our lives, and we agreed to end the relationship amicably. Ron moved away, which helped, but the only way people knew me around here was as Ron's girlfriend. It felt like I was starting all over again.

I'm telling you all this so you know that I understand maybe a little of how you felt during that hard transition after college.

In Him,
Angie

Hey Angie—
I'm glad that your faith is working for you. Reading your e-mail, it reminds me of the best of what college life was like.

Maybe I'm weaker than you are. I hated the loneliness and the confusion. And I hated it when those stupid college loan payments came due. All of those great words people said about my art talent being a gift from

God, and art being my calling, were just words. None
of those people were there to pay my bills or hire me to
do work for them.

I guess too many words, and too little action, turned
me off on Christianity the way we practiced it. I got
tired of sitting alone, reading my Bible and talking to
the ceiling, trying to get it right. Like you, I tried to find
a church right after college, but none of them seemed
to fit me. After a while, it was easier to stop trying.
None of my new friends went to church, and I needed
some friends pretty bad. Maybe I'm weaker than you, I
don't know.

But I really like my life now, and when I was trying to
be a Christian, I didn't.

Jessica

Hey Jessica—
Remember the time we drove all night just to go visit
Amy when she was in the hospital after her car accident?
I don't think I've ever laughed as hard as I did when you
decided to drive with a Krispy Kreme donut on your
head like it was a halo. I think the fact that it was four
in the morning probably made it a lot funnier than it
would have been any other time of day. I am laughing
as I'm typing, thinking about you driving eighty-five
with that donut balanced on your head. Remember the
little grease ring it left on your head after you took it
off and ate it?

The other thing I remember about that trip was how Amy looked lying there in that hospital bed. All those tubes, and the broken bones. Her whole life changed the day she fell asleep at the wheel heading back to school after spring break. She had to drop out, and it took her months to heal. She says now that the accident changed her life for the better.

It's hard to imagine how an accident like that could make anyone's life better, but she tells me now that she'd been living on the fence spiritually, and she really wasn't sure what she believed. I never would have known it at the time, would you? But she says that the accident slammed her off the fence and forced her into Jesus's arms. She's back in school now, almost done with a physical therapy degree. She says that the accident sent her down a completely different career path, as well as solidifying her commitment to Christ.

I'm telling you all this because I just heard that Amy will be coming to Jen's wedding. Another reason for you and Nate to reconsider! I know she'd love to see you. Everyone would, and they'd enjoy meeting Nate, too.

I promise—this will be the last hint I drop about you going.

In Him,
Angie

Hey Angie -
You're so sweet. Persistent, too. Yeah, it might be nice to see those people again. Ever since you first tracked me down a couple of weeks ago, I've been remembering all kinds of stuff about those college days. (Remember the time we tried making chili for the Super Bowl party, and it was so spicy that no one could eat it?) Our campus fellowship group was really like a family, the first decent one I'd ever known.

E-mailing you has made me wish I could go back in time and grab that lightning in a bottle. Everything seemed so simple then. Weird how different our lives are now.

Jessica

Hey Jessica—
I know what you mean. The relationships in our fellowship group were so sweet and intense. When I moved here and it was so hard and lonely, I discovered how much I'd depended on others to keep me going spiritually.

I tried different churches after I moved here, hoping to not feel lonely anymore, but I left each one feeling worse, like someone had wrapped me in Saran Wrap and placed me in a dark cabinet. I believed then, and I believe now, that Christianity isn't meant to be lived in isolation. You get weird when you're isolated.

The worst day was when I was sitting in a coffee shop alone after I'd visited yet another church. I started to cry, and no one noticed. Remember how Pastor Jim used to tell us all the time that tests show us what's really in our hearts, and that tests are really gifts? What a funny thing to tell college students, eh? But he was completely right.

Loneliness was my test. I realized how much I needed others to help me survive spiritually. It was a lightning bolt to discover that this need was what God intended—we're meant to live in community with others. A family, just like you said. And at the same time, I realized I needed to drill deeper into God's company before I'd have the wherewithal to reach out to others and need them without sucking them dry because I was terrified of being alone.

That's how I made it through, and that's how I'm still making it through.

In Him,
Angie

Angie—
I know you probably don't mean to make me feel like I've screwed up, but you have. It's the way Jen used to talk to me. The way you write, my confusion and loneliness were supposed to make me go deeper into God. What if it didn't, or I couldn't? What does that say about me? I'm sick of God talk.

Jessica

Hey Jessica—
What does it say about you? It says you're someone who God loves. I didn't mean to make you angry.

In Him,
Angie

Angie—
Even if I wanted to come back to God, I'm not sure I can. I've got a lot of baggage.

Jessica

Hey Jessica—
There's never too much baggage.

In Him,
Angie

Angie—
Nate just called me from work and told me that he wants to go out of town the weekend of the wedding. That solves the issue of us coming to the wedding, doesn't it?

I guess I won't be seeing you this time around. But stay in touch, okay?

Jessica

P.S.—Pray for me.

In Real Time

A couple of years ago, my husband Bill and I visited Arizona in August. You're probably wondering why anyone in their right mind would visit a desert in August. Well, we got a great deal on airfare (because no one in their right mind visits Arizona in August), so we went to see Bill's parents, who live out there.

It was good to see the fam, but it was like visiting them inside a giant oven. I would look at the thermometers on the bank clocks displaying temperatures as high as 118 degrees and I'd wonder if I was visiting Mars instead of Phoenix. In the Midwest, where we live, summer heat feels like a steaming washcloth is draped over the land. People kept saying things like "Arizona has dry heat" as if that makes 118 degrees more bearable. After a couple of days there, I concluded that 118 degrees isn't dry heat. It's hot heat.

During our visit, we decided to drive across the desert to check out the cactus and head toward the mountains up north. My in-laws informed us that a trip across the desert in the middle of August was not like jumping in the car and doing a quick run to Blockbuster to rent a movie. Being stranded on desolate, skillet-hot pavement—where there were few travelers and fewer cell phone towers available to relay a 911 call—forced us to do a little advance planning. We gassed up, we brought along a huge jug of "just in case" water for the radiator, and packed little bottles of iced drinking water. We learned that driving in the desert means keeping an eye on the car's temperature gauge, something we never need to do in the Midwest.

The commonsense steps we took were all about being prepared. We needed to plan our journey across the desert, and we needed to be prepared if our car broke down and our excursion switched from sightseeing to survival mode.

I remembered our trip prep when I thought about Jessica and Angie's choices after college. Both girls drove out into uncharted and inhospitable territory after college, and both of them experienced life breakdowns that left them feeling as stranded as they would have if they'd blown a radiator on a lonely road in the hot Arizona sun. Life breakdowns can be the loss of a decent roommate who paid half the rent or the challenge of finding meaningful employment with a hard-to-market degree. Life breakdowns can be relocating to a strange new place or losing a significant other who was helping you shape your new life there.

When you're stranded by a breakdown, you must rely on the preparations you made (or didn't make) before you left for your trip.

I don't want to oversimplify the route Angie's and Jessica's lives have taken. They had different childhoods, different personalities, different giftings. Those differences are significant and important, and those differences can account for some of the choices each made about how they were going to live their lives.

However, both young women shared the same basic opportunity to prepare both academically and spiritually for their life journeys during college. The preparation left them with the choice of what (if any) emergency reserves they were going to carry with them into their adulthood for the "just in case" life breakdown.

They are, in fact, not so different from the bridesmaids in Jesus's story. Their preparation (or lack thereof) left them unprepared for the bridegroom who showed up for the wedding in the middle of the night.

What Jesus says plainly, forcefully, and lovingly about the end of things in Matthew 24 is illuminated with the stories he told that explain how to best prepare for this journey. Besides the parable of the bridesmaids (Mt 25:1–13), Jesus tells another story about the way that three servants chose to invest some funds on behalf of the boss (Mt 25:14–30). Matthew 25 comes to a sober conclusion as Jesus explains how our preparation plays itself out for all eternity—life forever for those who've followed him as sheep faithfully follow their shepherd; fire and hell's torment for those who look like sheep but simply … aren't.

Jesus longs for us to wait, prepared for every "just in case" on the journey, for his return. He tells us we can best prepare by investing our energy in the things close to his heart: "For I was hungry and you gave me something to eat, I was thirsty and you gave me something to drink, I was a stranger and you invited me in, I needed clothes and you clothed me, I was sick and you looked after me, I was in prison and you came to visit me" (Mt 25:35–36).

What he's not saying is that if we do enough community service, we'll have an ironclad fire insurance policy. He is telling us that a waiting, prepared heart is watching for and responding to him, always, everywhere. And when he returns, those waiting will be ready for the wedding he's planned for those who've lived in love with him.

Please take some time to soak in the urgent message that's found in Matthew 24 and 25. Ask God to evaluate your life with you as you read. Are you draining your "just in case" reserves on here-and-now events? How? Are you prepared to follow him each step of the journey?

It is his joy to teach you to follow him. All you have to do is ask, and be ready to act on what you hear.

Continue the Conversation:
Waiting and preparing aren't individual exercises. There is a powerful corporate component to the wait, culminating in the wedding between a pure bride, the community of believers who are readying themselves, and Jesus, the Bridegroom (Rv 19:1–9). Is your church living as a waiting community, preparing for the feast? Why or why not?

CHAPTER TWELVE

One More Thing

Being His Story

I've tried to instruct my kids that God doesn't always give us what we want in our lives; he gives us what we need. The once-radical, now-corporate, Rolling Stones lyrics say the same thing, but they were just riffing on a truth that has been around for hundreds of generations.

When I delivered this inspiring message to my kids in the past, it was often in the cereal aisle of the grocery store, the one that looks like a comic strip because of all of those krazy and kolorful cereal boxes. I would choose inexpensive and nutritious breakfast foods like oatmeal and Raisin Bran. The kids, however, wanted the cartoons in a box: Cap'n Crunch, Froot Loops, and Cocoa Puffs.

This is when my 'God gives us what we need' sermonette came in handy. "Man does not live by processed sugar and empty carbs alone," I would add.

I would illustrate my powerful message by telling them for the 1,371st time that I, for one, have always wanted a pony, but that God, in his wisdom, has never given me one. We'd always lived in the wilds of densely packed suburbia, in tract housing or poorly constructed apartments. God knew we had nowhere to keep a pony. We also knew nothing about feeding a pony. (Maybe ponies like Cap'n Crunch. I really didn't know.)

At the exact moment that one or more of the kids were on the verge of beserkicide in the presence of all of those cartoon-y cereal boxes I would trot out my pony lament.

Ah, the majesty of those grocery store sermons.

I found out on my fortieth birthday the impact this nag of a message had on Rachel, Ben, and Jacob when I opened their gift to me. Inside the box were three shocking pastel My Little Ponies—little plastic toy horses that came in neon color combinations like cotton candy blue and faux Barbie pink. Each child had spent some of his or her hard-earned change for a present that communicated their deep respect for my life-changing message to them.

"See? You got some ponies," Jacob told me.

So I did. Those darn ponies rode away with my best Mom Sermon punch line.

It is amazing how most of us tend to script the answers to our own prayers, thinking we know just what the answer will look like—a Shetland pony tied up in the parking lot of the apartment complex. A truckload of Froot Loops for the pony to eat.

We pray for a new job, and we expect a little slice of good-paying employment heaven on earth. We ask God for a child and expect to be blessed with a perfect, healthy, quiet baby in exactly nine months. We beseech him to restore fractured relationships, and we can almost hear the swell of the happy ending music just before the credits roll.

Most of us are a little surprised somehow that people missed Jesus when he was living among them, living this revolution. The people most committed to God's promise of a Messiah had so ritualized their obedience and relationship with Scripture that when the Word was right before their very eyes, living a life of pure, obedient love, almost everyone missed him. What they were looking for was a collage pieced together from their own expectations and the parts of Scripture that promised a king who was going to bring the kind of justice their hearts craved: Roman butt getting kicked.

Blinded by their expectations, deafened by the sound of their own voices speaking for God, most saw Jesus's astonishing demonstrations of miracles, deliverances, and healing as a detour away from their hope of a King who was going to fix everything.

A piece of the passage from Isaiah 6 that Jesus quotes to explain why he spoke in parables (Mt 13:10–17) is referenced in a completely different context in the gospel of John. John described the crowds who followed Jesus around Jerusalem in the days leading up to his arrest:

> *Even after Jesus had done all these miraculous signs in their presence, they still would not believe in him. This was to fulfill the word of Isaiah the prophet:*
> *"Lord, who has believed our message and to whom has the arm of the Lord been revealed?"*
> *For this reason they could not believe, because, as Isaiah says elsewhere:*

*"He has blinded their eyes and deadened their hearts,
so they can neither see with their eyes, nor understand
with their hearts, nor turn—and I would heal them."
   Isaiah said this because he saw Jesus's glory and spoke
about him.*

—John 12:37–41

Jesus gave those blinded, heart-dead people the gift
they truly wanted—a lifeless box constructed of their own
expectations about God that trapped them inside like a
tomb.

The suffocating effects of religious subculture aren't the
only things that create boxes from expectations. Loss and
grief, abuse, loneliness, illness and our own stubborn choices
can build boxes that isolate us from God and each other. I
love what one friend said to me after admitting she'd grown
weary of the artificial confines of her box (constructed, in her
own words, out of too much fear about what "everyone else
would think" if she began living a life of kingdom-revolution
instead of her dry, overcooked church life): "You couldn't
limit God even if you tried. You can't put God in a box. He's
not in a box. *I am.*"

She's since taken the first wobbly steps out of the box and
into the heart of God. No map. No directions. Just one foot
in front of the other, following him.

Her unashamed desire for God is my confession, too. And
it just might be yours.

*I want to live with my eyes wide open,
   letting him fill my gaze everywhere I look.
I long to live with my ears tuned to the
   frequency of his communication with me,*

responding in surrender everywhere I go,
living his stories out loud.
I want to be healed with each step
I take toward him.
I want to live the parablelife.

What's your story?

What does it mean to you to live the ParableLife? Author Michelle Van Loon would love to hear how God's story is being written in your life. Please visit the ParableLife website to share your experiences, ask a question, or just say hey.

www.theparablelife.com

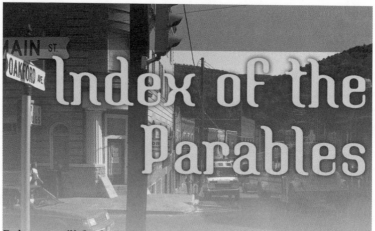

Index of the Parables

Below, you'll find a list of the parables contained in the gospels. The stories contained in this book are in bold print.

When compiling such lists, some Bible scholars combine some of the shorter parables that address the same theme (such as the found treasure and the pearl); others do not "count" the parables found in the gospel of John. I've listed them all. Use this list to help you discover the life-changing riches found in each of these amazing stories ... and the worth of the One who told the stories in the first place.

1. Salt—Matthew 5:13, Mark 9:50, Luke 14:34–35
2. **Two builders—Matthew 7:24–27, Luke 6:47–49**
3. **Children in the marketplace—Matthew 11:16-19; Luke 7:31–35**
4. Sower—Mathew 13:1–9, 18-23; Mark 4:1–9, 13–20; Luke 8:4–8, 11–15
5. Seed growing secretly—Mark 4:26–29
6. Wheat and weeds—Matthew 13:24–30, 36–43
7. Mustard seed—Matthew 13:31–32; Mark 4:30–32; Luke 13:18–19

8. Yeast—Matthew 13:33; Luke 13:20–21
9. **Found treasure—Matthew 13:44**
10. **Pearl—Matthew 13:45–46**
11. Net—Matthew 13:47–50
12. **Unforgiving servant—Matthew 18:21–35**
13. **Vineyard workers—Matthew 20:1–16**
14. Two sons—Matthew 21:28–32
15. Evil tenants—Matthew 21:33–46; Mark 12:1–12; Luke 20:9–19
16. Wedding banquet—Matthew 22:1–14
17. Fruitless fig tree—Luke 13:6–9
18. Sign of the fig tree—Matthew 24:32–35; Mark 13:28–31; Luke 21:29–33
19. Watching servant—Mark 13:32–27; Luke 12:35–38
20. Thief—Matthew 24:42–44; Luke 12:39–40
21. Servant with authority—Matthew 24:45–51; Luke 12:41–46
22. **Ten bridesmaids—Matthew 25:1–13**
23. Five, two, one talents–Matthew 25:14–30
24. Ten, five, one mina–Luke 19:11–27
25. Sheep and goats—Matthew 25:31–46
26. Two debtors—Luke 7:36–50
27. **Good Samaritan–Luke 10:25–37**
28. Friend at midnight—Luke 11:5–8
29. Rich fool—Luke 12:13–21
30. Places of honor—Luke 14:7–14
31. Calculating cost of a tower—Luke 14:28–29
32. Calculating cost of war—Luke 14:31–33
33. Lost sheep—Matthew 18:12–14; Luke 15:3–7
34. Lost coin—Luke 15:8–10
35. Lost son—Luke 15:8–10
36. Shrewd manager—Luke 16:1–9

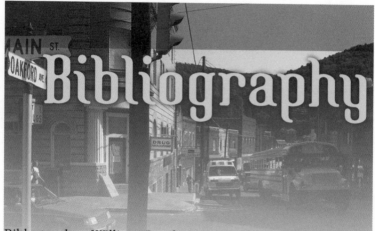

Bibliography

Bible teacher William Barclay noted that " ... parables are not carefully composed works of art, but sudden, lovely improvisations in the dust and heat of conflict." Some of the most transformational moments in my parablelife are being imparted to me in the same way.

Other moments of change have come as I've experienced the dust and heat of the ideas of others. I am indebted to the students of the Bible who have wrestled amazing insights from these lovely, true stories and have taken the time to write what they've discovered. The authors of these books have instructed me and challenged my thinking each step of my own mapless journey:

Barclay, William. *The Parables of Jesus* (Westminster John Knox, 1999)

Butler, Randy and Butler, Terry. "At the Cross." (Mercy/Vineyard Publishing, 1993)

Gustin, Marilyn. *How to Read and Pray the Parables* (Ligouri, 1992)

IVP New Testament Commentaries for Matthew and Luke (published by Intervarsity Press, accessible online at www.biblegateway.com)

Kalas, J. Ellsworth. *Parables from the Back Side: Bible Stories With a Twist* (Abingdon, 1992)

Kendall, R.T. *The Complete Guide to the Parables* (Chosen/Baker, 2004)

Kistemaker, Simon J. *The Parables: Understanding the Stories Jesus Told* (Baker, 1980)

Wenham, David. *The Parables of Jesus* (InterVarsity Press, 1980)

About the Author

Michelle Van Loon is a spiritual seeker wandering through the landscape of contemporary culture. She brings a mix of whip-smart secular Jewish heritage, thoughtful evangelical study, and hair-raising church experiences to her intensely honest writing. Van Loon is the author of three theatrical plays, numerous published articles, skits, and educational curriculum. She and her family live near Chicago, Illinois.

Michelle is a creative and passionate communicator, committed to encouraging people to see and hear God's story being written in their lives. If you're interested in having Michelle speak to your group, contact her at michelle@theparablelife.com.